CLEAN PLATES

Los Angeles 2015

A Guide to the
Healthiest, Tastiest
and Most Sustainable
Restaurants for Vegetarians
and Carnivores

By JARED KOCH

WITH CONTRIBUTIONS BY ASHLEY SPIVAK

DISCLAIMER: I am not a medical doctor, and nothing in this book is intended to diagnose, treat or cure any medical condition, illness or disease. Anyone with a specific medical condition should consult a physician.

© 2014 Jared Koch

All rights reserved. No part of this book may be reproduced or transmitted in any form or by any means, electronic or mechanical, including photocopying, recording or by any information storage and retrieval system, without permission in writing from the publisher.

Published by Clean Plates
Palisades Park, NJ

Interior design by Gary Robbins

Printed in Canada

10   9   8   7   6   5   4   3   2   1

Library of Congress
Cataloging-in-Publication Data:

Koch, Jared.
　　Clean Plates Los Angeles 2015: A Guide
　　to the Healthiest, Tastiest and Most
　　Sustainable Restaurants for Vegetarians
　　and Carnivores / by Jared Koch. –
　　Palisades Park, NJ : Clean Plates, 2014.
　　p.　cm.
　　ISBN 978-0-9859221-9-1
　　1. Food—Popular works.
　　2. Diet—Popular works.
　　3. Nutrition—Popular works.
　　4. Restaurants—California
　　　　—Los Angeles.
　　I. Title.
TX355.K63   2014
641—dc22
2008940260

CONTENTS

WHAT IS CLEAN PLATES?

THE FIVE KEYS TO CLEAN EATING

THE CLEAN PLATES 100 LA RESTAURANTS

WHAT IS CLEAN PLATES?

A NOTE FROM JARED

For first-timers, I am excited to introduce you to Clean Plates. For those already familiar, I am thrilled to have you join us again. *Clean Plates LA* highlights the top 100 healthiest, tastiest and most sustainable restaurants in Los Angeles.

Let's face it: We dine out a lot, and restaurants can be bad-eating minefields. But eating healthier does not have to be challenging. No one actually wants to consume hormones, antibiotics or pesticides, it's just that searching for the good stuff takes time. That's where *Clean Plates LA* comes in. We've done all the dirty work for you to make clean eating an easy, pleasurable and sacrifice-free adventure.

Clean Plates LA is about helping you make better, more informed choices. Sure, there's a lot of nutritional information out there, but it can be totally confusing. That's why, along with the Clean Plates 100 LA restaurants, this guide provides an easy-to-follow overview of how to best eat clean while dining out.

By now you're probably asking yourself: Who is this guy? Why should I listen to anything he says? Well, honestly, I'm not that different from you. I want to be healthy so I can enjoy my life and contribute to making the world a better place. Rather than bore you with a long report about my background (you can learn more by visiting cleanplates.com), I'll touch on a few highlights for your peace of mind.

After deferring my acceptance to medical school for a decade-long stint as a successful entrepreneur, I decided that I needed to focus on my health and happiness. As part of that journey, I not only became a certified nutritional consultant but also healed myself from chronic irritable bowel syndrome (IBS), fatigue and skin issues. I have had some amazing teachers: Andrew Weil, M.D.; Deepak Chopra; Dr. Mark Hyman; and Walter Willett, the Chair of the Department of Nutrition at Harvard; in addition to many experts in the fields of raw foods, Chinese medicine, Ayurveda, macrobiotics, vegetarianism and high-protein diets. In this book, I synthesize a variety of dietary theories in an easy-to-use format— always keeping an open mind to discovering the truth about what actually works for each individual.

Thanks to my experiences, I've had several insights over the years about how we eat, which is the foundation on which Clean Plates has been built. I will share these insights with you throughout this guide.

I wrote this book because there is a real lack of helpful, well-organized information for people who wish to dine out mindfully and still enjoy the experience of eating. Sure, cooking at home is important, and many nutrition books (including *The Clean Plates Cookbook*, as well as our website cleanplates.com) offer delicious recipes, but the truth is, we eat out a lot— it is part of Los Angeles' culture. We created *Clean Plates LA* to be the most exceptionally well-researched, comprehensive and easy-to-use guide that exists. I am certain it will help you navigate the ever-expanding maze of LA's healthiest, tastiest and most sustainable restaurants.

Together, let's shatter the myth that healthier eating is a sacrifice and prove that we can do it without the guilt, inconvenience, boredom and sheer lack of long-term success that characterize the usual diets. You see, eating clean food is admirable, but I am equally interested in clean plates— the kind of food that makes you want to lick the dishes.

In good health,

WHY EAT CLEAN

CLEAN PLATES' MISSION is to make it easy and enjoyable for you to eat better. The first step is simply reminding yourself why you want to focus on your eating habits in the first place. There are a multitude of reasons why you may decide to eat better; at the end of the day it all comes down to choices. Here are some reasons to help you choose wisely and intentionally.

FOR PHYSICAL HEALTH AND QUALITY OF LIFE

Our health may be affected more by the foods we eat than by any other factor. This is great news, since it means we can do something about it. Of course, exercise, sleep and genetics—not to mention our relationships, career and spirituality—count, too. But the reason "you are what you eat" has endured as a phrase is because what we consume builds, fuels, cleanses or—unfortunately—pollutes our very cells.

If you're healthy, you're more likely to:

- have more energy to enjoy life and live to your fullest potential;
- enjoy greater mental clarity for work and play;
- maintain emotional equilibrium and a pleasant mood;
- suffer from fewer minor ailments such as colds and allergies;
- reduce your risk of contracting potentially fatal diseases like cancer, diabetes and heart disease;
- age more slowly and gracefully, staving off problems like arthritis and Alzheimer's disease;
- save money by having fewer healthcare bills and less time off work;
- have clearer skin and a trimmer physique (a little vanity never hurt anyone).

FOR THE WORLD BEYOND YOUR PLATE

Here's a new one: An organic apple a day keeps the greenhouse gases away. Translation? Eating clean is good for nature. When you start choosing cleaner foods, you can positively affect the planet. When you choose grass-fed meats, you are supporting farmers who employ humane practices. When you choose non-GMO certified products you are taking a stand against the enormous amount of pesticides it takes to grow GMO crops and the adverse effects of cross-contamination on both the land and wildlife.

And the icing on the cake (naturally sweetened, of course)? When we choose eco-friendly practices, most of the time it is also healthier for us.

CLEAN PLATES: MORE THAN JUST THIS GUIDE

SIGN UP FOR OUR EMAIL

Visit cleanplates.com and sign up to receive nutritional tips, recipes and behind-the-scene looks at your favorite Clean Plates establishments and chefs.

VISIT CLEANPLATES.COM

While this guide features the Clean Plates 100 LA restaurants, our website showcases more than 1,000 establishments that emphasize clean eating and sustainability. Explore cleanplates.com for national content or browse by city (LA and New York City) for hundreds of restaurant reviews plus articles packed with food scene news, chef interviews, healthy eating tips, product picks, recipes and more.

DOWNLOAD OUR IPHONE APP

Our iPhone app with geolocation makes clean eating choices on the go—from fine dining to quick farm-to-fork eats—easier than ever. Choose from hundreds of restaurants based on location, cuisine or dietary needs.

BUY OUR COOKBOOK

Available at Amazon.com, Barnes and Noble and local retailers, *The Clean Plates Cookbook* offers sensible, sustainable and healthful home cooking tips and recipes for anyone interested in maintaining a clean lifestyle while dining in.

HOW TO USE THIS GUIDE

JUST AS THERE'S no one-size-fits-all diet for everyone, there's no one right way to read and use this book. But here are several helpful features.

TAKE IT WITH YOU EVERYWHERE

Constructed to be small and lightweight, *Clean Plates LA* is easy to slip in a bag or back pocket, and its rounded corners will keep it from getting dog-eared. No matter where you are in LA, you'll be able to quickly locate a restaurant that serves a healthy, delicious version of the cuisine you're in the mood for—from fast food to fine dining, vegan to BBQ and any combination thereof. Don't want to keep it on you? Store one at home and one at the office. (Hey, we won't stop you from buying two.)

LEARN MORE ABOUT CLEAN EATING

Check out the "Clean Plates Philosophy" section, preceding the restaurant reviews, where we outline the Five Keys to Clean Eating. This section provides an easy-to-follow education on how to best eat clean while dining out so you have a foundation from which you can make intelligent and informed choices to implement healthier eating habits immediately.

FIND YOUR PERFECT MATCH

We don't want anyone to be left out. So whether you're a vegetarian or meat-eater, want to eat gluten-free or not—and whether you want to spend lavishly or lightly—we've tracked down restaurants for you (always serving delicious meals, naturally). *Clean Plates LA* boasts an incredibly diverse array of establishments (including full reviews) representing many different cuisines, budgets and geographic locations. There are many ways to find your perfect match:

BY ICON We have created special icons to indicate the restaurant's price point, whether it offers grab-and-go options, and/or delivery and whether the establishment offers gluten-free, vegetarian/vegan choices, and/or specializes in thoughtfully procured animal proteins. See p. 65 for our icon key. You can search this book by icon using the index beginning on p. 176.

ALPHABETICALLY Restaurant reviews are presented alphabetically in this guide.

THE INDEX The index lets you quickly find what you are looking for in a variety of configurations—search by icons, geography, and even specific social situations like Brunch and Business Lunch. See p. 176.

TOP FIVES This year we've included the Top Fives page (p. 66) to help you easily find our favorite picks for specific dietary wants and needs like vegetarian/vegan and Paleo-friendly.

BEYOND RESTAURANTS Check out our favorite places to grab some organic pastries, fair-trade coffee, clean food-truck fare, ice cream, cold-pressed juice and artisanal provisions (p. 167).

DISCOVER HOW EATING WELL CAN BE FUN, STRESS-FREE AND LIFE-CHANGING

Use this guide to help you effortlessly eat healthier—since Clean Plates does the work for you—and put to rest the excuse that healthy foods are too inaccessible and expensive to incorporate into your life. When you start eating better food, you'll begin craving it and your body will respond by rewarding you with better moods, energy and health.

HOW WE CHOOSE THE RESTAURANTS

OVER THE YEARS Los Angeles has become rich with options for clean dining. What you have in your hands is a one-of-a-kind guide to the 100 best of the best restaurants in LA serving healthier dishes that pleased our food critics' discerning palates.

Our goal was to compile a wide-ranging list of healthy LA restaurants that accommodated both vegetarians and carnivores to meet your needs under many circumstances. We scoured other guidebooks, newsletters and websites, petitioned chefs and restaurateurs, and drove all over the city looking for discerning candidates. This produced a list of 500 restaurants! From there we subjected each restaurant on our master list to a health-screening process. Posing as a potential customer over the phone, we queried the staff about their preparation and sourcing methods. (Is your meat hormone- and antibiotic-free? Is it grass-fed? What is your apple pie sweetened with?) In addition, we thoroughly reviewed the menu online and in person.

If the restaurant passed this initial health test, we sent a survey to the chef, general manager or restaurant owner to gather even more specific information about ingredients and sourcing practices. Metrics were created to evaluate their responses, and our amazing food critics and writers—Rachel Levin, Elisa Huang and Zoe Alexander —were sent to assess the highest-scoring establishments incognito to avoid special treatment.

A wide variety of food was ordered—appetizers, side dishes, main courses and desserts. In addition, the staff was asked more questions, both to fact-check our initial queries and to gather more information.

Then, we sat down and assessed the restaurant from an editorial perspective (see what we took into consideration below). Again, our goal was to not only provide you with the healthiest, tastiest and most sustainability-focused restaurants, but to also provide as much variety as possible. True, we may have missed a few—this is LA after all, home to a dizzying array of eateries—but we tried to make it as comprehensive as possible.

Please note, we are not operating as a certifying agency. We have curated this guide to bring you an assortment of options based upon what we think will be most useful for a typical LA lifestyle.

When choosing a restaurant, we took the following into account:

TASTE Part of the Clean Plates mission is to prove that healthy eating doesn't mean sacrificing taste. Therefore, we sent experienced food critics to each restaurant to ensure your taste buds will be as satisfied as your body.

ATMOSPHERE Whether you need a quick fix in the middle of the workday, are trying to impress a date or are looking to be pampered, we were sure to include a variety of establishments to meet all needs.

GEOGRAPHY Wherever you live, work, shop and hang out, we've identified a restaurant nearby that serves healthy and delicious meals. We tried to offer suggestions in as many parts of the city as we could.

CUISINE From Italian to Indian, French to gastropub, we tried our best to have you covered.

PRICE It was important to us to include restaurants in all price ranges, from less than $15 for a full meal to more than $60.

INGREDIENT SOURCING AND SUSTAINABILITY PRACTICES We look for restaurants that are transparent with their sourcing practices for animal products and produce, buy locally when possible, have a focus on organic ingredients, use high-quality cooking oils, salts and sweeteners, and don't have a large percentage of deep-fried foods on the menu. We also look for establishments that compost, filter their water, recycle, and are part of third-party associations such as City Harvest, the Green Restaurant Association and the Slow Food movement.

MENU OFFERINGS We believe that meals are meant to bring people together. Therefore we emphasize restaurants that offer vegetable-based *and* meat-centric dishes so that those with different dietary preferences can still dine together. We also look for establishments that cater to specific dietary needs like gluten-free and vegan.

If you stick to eating at these restaurants when you dine out, there's a good chance you'll improve your quality of life and your health. Why? For one thing, you'll be putting better foods into your body, and it will respond in kind. For another, you'll start to associate delicious meals with healthy meals— and you'll begin to crave the latter. Consuming junk food will seem less and less appealing. And you'll be doing all of this with little effort because the restaurants—and this guide—will have done the work for you. All you have to do is eat!

THE CLEAN PLATES PHILOSOPHY:
THE FIVE KEYS TO CLEAN EATING

1

There's more than one right way to eat.

We believe there is a dream diet for everyone—but it's not the same for each person. As nutrition pioneer Roger Williams wrote in his groundbreaking 1950s book *Biochemical Individuality*, "If we continue to try to solve problems on the basis of the average man, we will be continually in a muddle. Such a man does not exist."

We're all biochemically—genetically, hormonally and so on— different, and the idea that this should guide our eating habits has recently begun to excite the leading-edge medical and nutrition community. Experts are beginning to talk about the benefits of individualizing our diets rather than giving advice based on recommended daily allowances (RDA) or the U.S. Department of Agriculture's "My Plate," both created with the "average" person in mind.

EATING AS A BIO-INDIVIDUAL

The philosophy that no single way of eating is right for everyone isn't new. Both traditional Chinese medicine and India's Ayurvedic system revolve around prescribing the most appropriate diet for specific categories of body types and constitutions.

More recent incarnations of these ancient approaches include the blood-type diet and metabolic typing. The blood-type diet was made famous more than a decade ago by naturopath Peter D'Adamo, who theorized (to put it very simply) that people with type O blood do best eating meat, while those with type A thrive as vegetarians. The thinking behind the discovery? Those with type O descended from ancient hunters while those with type A came from agricultural civilizations. The idea behind metabolic typing (again, to put it simply) is that your metabolism dictates the appropriate percentage of proteins and carbohydrates in your diet. Those who metabolize proteins well require extra animal foods, while others do better with more carbs.

Not everyone takes the bio-individual approach. For example, proponents of *The China Study*, a 2005 book by two nutritional biochemists who conducted a 20-year survey of Chinese diets, argue that animal consumption is the leading cause of human disease and everyone would be better off if they cut back, while followers of Weston A. Price, a dentist who carried out extensive health research in many countries, rely on culturally based studies to back up their claim that animal proteins and organ meats have benefits. They suggest everyone would be better off incorporating more animal foods into their diet.

As you read through the list below of how we're all unique, some of the points may seem obvious. (Of course someone training for a marathon requires different foods than someone sitting in front of a computer all day, for instance.) But these distinctions manifest not only between individuals, but also between your different selves—your tired self, your active self and the like. Eating as a bio-individual means paying attention to how your body reacts to various foods and assessing for yourself how your unique body best thrives.

HOW WE DIFFER

GENETIC MAKEUP To a large extent, the anatomy and body chemistry you inherited from your ancestors determines your nutritional needs and ability to benefit from particular foods. For example, a few recent studies have shown that some people possess the genetic ability to metabolize caffeine more efficiently than others. Research has also revealed that specific groups of people have the genetic makeup to absorb vitamin B12 with ease, or benefit greatly from broccoli's cancer-fighting nutrients, while others lack that ability.

CULTURE AND BACKGROUND Your ethnicity and upbringing can influence how your body acts. For instance, many people whose families come from Asia are lactose intolerant. It's helpful to consider which foods are part of your culture and background and incorporate the appropriate ones into your diet.

LIFESTYLE You require different foods when training for a marathon than when you practice an hour of yoga each week.

DAY-TO-DAY PHYSICAL HEALTH Pay attention to your physical health symptoms to figure out what foods you need. Sick? Miso soup may be just the thing. Sneezing constantly? Avoid dairy and sugar; the former causes the body to produce mucus and the latter weakens the immune system.

GENDER Your gender affects your diet needs. For example, menstruating women require more iron than men, but men need more zinc than women to nourish their reproductive systems.

AGE A growing, active teen will be ravenous at dinnertime. The same person, 60 years later, will likely find that his appetite is waning.

SEASONS AND CLIMATE Even the weather affects what's best for you to eat. When it's hot outside, the body will likely crave cooling foods like salads; on a cold winter day, hot soup is more appealing.

HOW WE'RE THE SAME

Our food choices often become another way of separating us. When there are moral underpinnings to our choices, it's especially tempting to think "My way is the only right way to eat." While bio-individuality may seemingly highlight how we are different, these distinctions are only made to reach a shared goal—to thrive physically. Once this has been achieved, we've created an unshakable foundation for living to our fullest potential and for making a meaningful contribution to our collective well-being as a species and a planet.

Being different should bring us together. Why? Partially because it's about realizing that other people have needs distinct from ours. Some types love to begin their day with a shot of wheatgrass— but perhaps the thought makes you turn green. While your friends can't imagine living without an occasional hamburger or slice of pizza, you might thrive on hearty salads and raw foods. And we all know that irritating person who can gobble up everything in sight and remain slim—a profile that many of us don't have. Hopefully being aware of these distinctions will lead us to be less critical of others— and less likely to feel guilty about our own choices. Judgment and guilt, after all, are bad for your health. At the very least, they really mess with your digestion.

HOW SHOULD YOU APPROACH OTHER DIETARY THEORIES?

One diet (it's a stretch to call it a dietary theory!) that most of us would like to move away from is the standard American diet (aka SAD). So what should we move toward? We all have different needs, but that doesn't mean we have to invent diets from scratch. We have help: other established dietary theories.

Think of it as designing your own diet using bits and pieces of good, but different ideas, gathered from a variety of established theories. The point is that you don't need to adhere to any particular theory; each has its pros and cons, and none is right for everyone. Instead, tailor what you eat to your biology, body, hormones, tastes and way of looking at the world. The Five Keys to Clean Eating will help to guide your choices.

Bio-individuality means there is no perfect diet for everyone. There is, however, the perfect food for everyone—real food. It's what we're designed to eat, regardless of our lifestyle, genetic makeup and other differences. Which leads to the next Key to Clean Eating.

#2

The overwhelming majority of your diet should consist of natural, high-quality and whole foods.

WHICH MEANS ... WHAT? What, exactly, is real food? Once upon a time it had an obvious answer, but, over the past hundred years, food has become increasingly unlike itself: processed, altered with chemicals, dyed unnatural colors, flavored with suspect ingredients and turned as artificial as can be. These kinds of changes generally result in more toxins and fewer nutrients. The success of diets like Paleo, macrobiotics and raw foods in claiming to help heal diabetes and even cancer (according to some studies) is due in large part to the fact that these diets call for increasing your intake of real, high quality, whole foods while reducing consumption of artificial and chemical-laden dishes.

TIP: DON'T GET SIDETRACKED BY FOCUSING ONLY ON CALORIES

Many people equate reducing calories with a healthier lifestyle, but Clean Plates firmly believes that the quality of the foods we eat are much more important—even when it comes to losing weight. Here's a way of looking at it: Think of food as fuel. Does a car run best on poor-quality fuel? Of course not. Our bodies are the same: They need optimal fuel. Another way of looking at it is to ask yourself: What's better for my body—a 150-calorie candy bar or 200 calories of vegetables?

All this means we desperately need to get back to the basics. So, what exactly is real food?

REAL/NATURAL FOODS

In this guide the terms 'real' and 'natural' are used synonymously to denote foods that are neither highly processed nor artificial. Knowing what's natural is largely a matter of intuition and common sense; it's not as if you're going to start bringing a checklist to restaurants.

Nevertheless, you'll become a pro at identifying the real thing more quickly if you ask yourself a couple of questions the next time you eat: What would I eat if I lived in the wild? What has the earth and nature provided for humans to eat? What have I, as a human, evolved to eat? To keep it simple, focus on what grows out of the ground or on a tree. In addition, think vegetables, fruits, nuts, seeds, beans, grains, herbs and animal foods.

TIP: AN EASY WAY TO FIGURE OUT IF IT'S REAL FOOD

Ask yourself this question: Was it made in nature or in a factory? Visualize where the item began its life. Perhaps you'll see it hanging on a bush, growing on a tree, sprouting up from the earth or grazing in a field. If it's fizzing to life in a test tube, move on.

NOT ALL REAL/NATURAL FOODS ARE EQUAL

While the goal is to incorporate as many real foods into the diet as possible, there are a few things to think about to ensure you are getting the most out of your food.

IS IT A WHOLE FOOD?

Generally speaking, the less heat, pressure and processing a food is exposed to, the more whole it is. But this doesn't necessarily mean we should only consume raw foods. For some foods the nutrients are most bioavailable in their raw state; for others, some exposure to low heat actually breaks down the food's cell walls and fiber, making it easier for our bodies to absorb the nutrients.

Because there are benefits to consuming both cooked and raw foods, we should aim to incorporate both into our diets. The ratio will ultimately depend on the strength of your digestive system and personal tastes.

When examining the wholeness of a prepared dish, you should consider:

- The cooking methods used. Err on the side of undercooking, since prolonged exposure to high heat destroys nutrients, enzymes and water content. Examples: Steaming or poaching (good) versus boiling (not good) or deep frying (bad).
- The ingredients. Examples: A bowl of berries (good) versus fruit juice with sugar (not good).
- The number of steps or processes used to make the food. Examples: A bowl of oatmeal made from steel-cut oats (good) versus cereal made into flakes (not so good).

IS IT A HIGH QUALITY FOOD?

A peach from the grocery store is a real-food item—it was made in nature and wasn't flavored in a factory—but that doesn't mean it's the best quality. There's a difference if that peach was irradiated and artificially ripened or if that peach was grown organically and locally. In the former, you'd be ingesting produce with an altered chemical structure, fewer nutrients and more pesticides, whereas in the latter you'd be ingesting chemical-free, highly nutritious, fresh fruit.

In addition, ask yourself if additives, flavorings, coloring or preservatives were used. It's not always obvious in a restaurant, but it's worth considering. For instance, are those fresh peaches in your pie, or are they from a can?

WHAT'S MORE IMPORTANT: LOCALLY GROWN OR ORGANIC?

Organic but non-local produce is free of pesticides harmful to our bodies and the soil, but it requires extra energy to travel from farm-to-table and loses nutrients along the way. Locally grown but non-organic goods retain most of their nutrients because of the speed at which they get to our plates, but they may be sprayed with chemicals that are damaging to our bodies, the soil and the atmosphere.

If you can't get an item locally grown *and* organic, there is no easy answer. It is a matter of personal choice, and if you choose one or the other you are doing pretty good.

TIP: A WORD OF CAUTION

Just because locally grown and organic foods are better for the environment doesn't mean they're always healthier for our bodies. Locally grown, organic sugar? Sorry, it's still sugar to your body.

Confusion and controversy surround many types of food. In the following sections we'll go a bit more in depth about the different food groups to help you make more informed choices when ordering off a menu.

#3

Everyone would be better off if a larger proportion of their diet consisted of plants—mostly vegetables (in particular, leafy greens), along with some nuts, seeds and fruits.

OK, so you've heard this many times before and still can't help but snooze when you hear "Eat more plants"? Maybe telling yourself "I'll have more energy" will provide the necessary motivation, because when we eat plant foods we are consuming the best energy there is.

To get this message to sink in, think about it in big, overarching terms. Eating plants is a way of taking in energy from the sun. As a life force, the sun makes an enormous contribution to our health and sense of well-being. Without it there would be no life on earth. Want more of it? Eat more plants. Unlike animal foods, plants are a direct source of "sun food."

If this concept is too esoteric, consider it from a scientific point of view. What gives green plants their color? It's chlorophyll, the pigment in leaves that enables them to absorb the sun's rays using a process called photosynthesis. Many nutritionists believe that when we eat green leaves, we take in that stored solar energy. Chlorophyll enriches blood, kills germs, detoxifies the bloodstream and liver, reduces bodily odors, and controls the appetite.

To help you navigate between different types of plants, the following two sections of this book are devoted to information about vegetables and fruits. It's not wrong to eat meat—in fact, it can be healthy—but eat lots of plants and you'll start to feel better. The next two sections show you why.

VEGGIE TALES

Pity the unappreciated vegetable. Perpetually shunted to the side—as a garnish, appetizer, side dish—it rarely gets to give all that it has to offer. What does it offer, you ask? An enormous amount of nutrients and health-boosting properties in the form of vitamins, minerals, fiber, phytochemicals and antioxidants. Vegetables should form the bulk of your diet.

QUICK DEFINITION: ANTIOXIDANTS

Their name says it all: they're anti-oxidants. They counteract oxidation and the free radicals believed to speed up aging and disease. A variety of elements cause our bodies to produce excess free radicals, ranging from toxic air and the chemicals to which we're exposed, to the normal process of metabolizing food for energy. Fortunately, you can combat these excess free radicals by eating more vegetables (as well as fruits, nuts and seeds), which are abundant in antioxidants.

If you're a vegetarian, aim to increase the proportion of veggies that you consume relative to the amount of grains, beans, dairy, sugar and tofu in your diet. Similarly, omnivores should be mindful of the meat-to-vegetable ratio in each meal.

TIP: CROWD OUT THE BAD STUFF

The concept is simple: The more vegetables we eat, the less room we'll have for junk foods and the like. Just one extra helping of veggies a day crowds out one helping of unhealthy food, a fact that proves motivating when making dietary changes. Instead of trying to avoid bad foods, focus on eating more vegetables. You'll actually start craving them. Meanwhile, the junk will slowly become less appealing.

Remember to eat high-quality, natural and whole vegetables. They taste noticeably better, and local, organic vegetables tend to reap the benefits of healthier soils as well as suffer less nutrient loss than their long-distance counterparts.

To help you order at restaurants, here's a roundup of the types of vegetables you're likely to encounter on menus—and how they affect your body:

GREENS should be a priority because they're among the most nutrient-dense foods. Chock-full of chlorophyll, they also boast a calcium-to-magnesium ratio that makes them great bone builders and encourages relaxation and appropriate nerve-and-muscle responsiveness, ensuring the body's smooth functioning. They are also a good way to obtain iron, vitamin C and folate. Let's take a look at some of the more common leafy greens:

Kale, swiss chard, collards and spinach are all chef favorites. If possible, ask for yours to be lightly steamed or even served raw, both options that retain more nutrients than a long sauté. A quick sauté with olive oil and garlic is another delicious and healthy alternative. Spinach is probably the most familiar of leafy greens (thanks, Popeye!) but we encourage you to incorporate all types of leafy greens into your diet as spinach contains oxalic acid which some research shows could prevent proper nutrient absorption (but not enough that we recommend you avoid it all together).

Lettuce, mesclun greens, watercress and arugula often appear in salads and are a great way to get your raw-food fill. Watercress in particular is rich in B vitamins.

Parsley and dandelion greens, both highly nutritious, don't make it onto menus as often as other greens, except as a garnish. If you do see them on the menu, try them. They are both incredibly rich in iron and vitamin C, and great for liver and kidney health.

Wheatgrass tends to conjure up images of earthy-crunchy types, but its health benefits beg you to look past this visual. It boasts one of the most concentrated sources of chlorophyll, a pigment (as you may recall from earlier) that captures the sun's energy and passes its healthful effects along to your body. Visit a juice bar (see p. 172) or health food restaurant and knock it back like a shot of the finest espresso.

CRUCIFEROUS VEGETABLES are plants in the cabbage family, a category that includes, to name a few, broccoli, cauliflower, Brussels sprouts, kale, bok choy and all cabbages (yes, there's some overlap with the leafy greens group). High in vitamin C and soluble fiber, these foods also are crammed with nutrients boasting potent anti-cancer properties. They are especially high in vitamin K, which plays an important role in the inflammation response. Only cruciferous vegetables contain isothiocyanates, nutrients that have been associated with a decrease in cancer.

ROOT VEGETABLES include carrots, beets, potatoes, parsnips, yams, turnips and radishes, each with a unique nutritional profile. Carrots and sweet potatoes, for instance, contain the antioxidant betacarotene, which helps prevent against free radicals; beets contain betalain, a unique antioxidant that acts as an anti-inflammatory and nurtures eye health and nerve tissue support.

TIP: THE INSTA-NUTRIENT SHOT

Drinking the juice of any type of green—not just wheatgrass—is a speedy way to get a nutrient infusion without your teeth or digestive system having to work at breaking down the plants' cell walls. Nevertheless, don't stop eating whole greens, since they provide fiber as well as some nutrients that may be lost or oxidized in the juicing process.

MUSHROOMS, which are actually fungi, not vegetables, probably generate the most controversy, at least as far as their health claims go. Some nutritionists advise steering clear because they are, after all, a type of fungus, and are therefore potentially infectious. They're also hard to digest when consumed raw. Other experts, however, particularly those who study Asian cultures, vaunt the medicinal properties of mushrooms. We suggest sticking with the shiitake and maitake (hen of the woods) varieties, both of which have cancer-fighting and immune-boosting properties. (Recent studies suggest that portobella mushrooms may lead to weight loss, and button mushrooms contain several goodies such as antioxidants, too.)

KIMCHI AND SAUERKRAUT are both raw and fermented veggies—the former served in Korean establishments and the latter in Eastern European restaurants. Literally "alive," they teem with nutrients, enzymes and probiotics, which aid digestion.

QUICK DEFINITION: PROBIOTICS AND ENZYMES

We hear it constantly: Such-and-such food boasts enzymes and probiotics. But what do those odd-sounding things do? Enzymes control the rate of every chemical reaction in your system, which means that you need them to digest food. So what happens when we don't get our enzymes, which are potentially destroyed by overcooking? Bad digestion. Probiotics are microorganisms that promote the growth of healthy bacteria in the gut that rid your intestines of the bad stuff. The upshot? You're healthier when you get probiotics.

SEAWEEDS, OR SEA VEGGIES, include nori (used to wrap sushi), hijiki, wakame, dulse and many others. Extremely dense in minerals, they add a salty, ocean-like taste to dishes and can often be found at Asian establishments and vegetarian eateries. Not familiar with this food? Try a seaweed salad or ask for extra in your miso soup; both are easy, delicious ways to familiarize yourself with sea veggies—and to enjoy a big, healthy dose of minerals.

THE RAINBOW RULE

It can be difficult to make sure you're getting the right balance of nutrients. Here's a good rule to follow: Eat as many different colors of vegetables each day as possible. Each pigment correlates to specific phytochemicals, all of which boost your immunity and act as health insurance against a range of nutrient deficiencies and diseases.

FEELING FRUITY

Think of fruits as sweets that are good for us! Fruits are good sources of fiber, antioxidants, phytochemicals and vitamins, and provide energy via easily digestible sugars. And don't be concerned about creating huge spikes in blood sugar; it's generally not an issue because fruits come packaged with fiber and other co-factors.

QUICK DEFINITION:

Co-factor: A co-factor is a nutrient that helps another nutrient work better.

As they should comprise a smaller percentage of your overall plant intake, it's fitting that fruit makes up a smaller percentage of plant foods offered at restaurants—vegetables pop up all over menus, but fruits tend to appear only in juices, smoothies or desserts.

Here are details about fruits you're likely to find on menus:

NON-SWEET FRUITS, such as peppers, tomatoes and cucumbers, rank low on the glycemic index and therefore barely disrupt our blood-sugar balance. During the summer, check out the many delicious varieties of locally grown heirloom tomatoes.

QUICK DEFINITION:
GLYCEMIC INDEX

This system is a way of
ranking a food's effect on
your body's blood sugar
level. Using the numbers
1 through 100, the lower
the number, the lesser
the impact and the lower
the chance of unhealthy
blood-sugar spikes.

QUICK TIP: SQUEEZE
SOME LEMON IN YOUR
WATER

Even though lemons taste
acidic, they're actually
one of the most alkalizing
foods as far as the
chemistry they produce in
your blood. So squeeze
some lemon in your
morning glass of water
for an alkalizing start to
your day.

FATTY FRUITS, such as avocadoes and olives, are arguably the best source of fats you can eat, because they are whole and come from plants (in contrast to many processed oils). Eaten raw, as they always should be, avocadoes and olives contain a fat-digesting enzyme, lipase, that makes them easy for our bodies to process.

BERRIES are a favorite sweet fruit, both from a culinary and nutritional perspective. On the glycemic index, they rank lowest of all the sweet fruits. Individually, each berry is touted for a specific attribute. For instance, blueberries offer significantly more vitamin K, while raspberries help to nourish the female reproductive system and provide fiber.

CITRUS FRUITS include oranges, lemons, limes and grapefruits. They tend to be high in immune-boosting vitamin C and in bioflavonoids—a type of antioxidant known for its anti-cancer properties, as well as its role in keeping blood capillaries healthy. Although citrus fruits taste acidic, they are, in fact, alkalizing and help to counteract the acidity of the meat, grains and beans that typically form the bulk of a restaurant meal.

ACID VS. ALKALINE

Let's travel back in time to your fifth grade science class. Remember learning about pH levels? A 7 on the 0-to-14 pH scale is neutral, with anything below considered acidic and anything above alkaline. Why is this relevant? Different foods create different byproducts in the metabolic process. Some foods, like animal products and processed foods, tend to cause more acidic residues, whereas others, like certain fruits and vegetables, create more alkaline residues. An acidic environment decreases the body's ability to absorb certain minerals and nutrients, inhibits the repair of damaged cells, causes inflammation, and hinders detoxification. Therefore, we want to consume less of the foods that create acidic residues and more of the foods that create alkaline residues for an optimal blood pH level.

ORCHARD FRUITS include apples, pears and peaches. Best eaten raw for their enzymes, fiber and nutrients, these fruits usually show up in fruit salads and smoothies.

TROPICAL FRUITS like papayas, mangoes and pineapples are especially rich in the kinds of enzymes that are not only powerful aids to digestion but also may help to break down scar tissue and waste materials in the body. They offer a tasty alternative to refined sugar for someone craving a sweet snack.

GRAINS

Many people consider a fresh-baked loaf of bread, or pasta with tomatoes and garlic, a bit of an indulgence—OK when eaten infrequently, but to be avoided in large quantities. And we agree. If you tolerate them well, grains can add fiber, protein, other nutrients and enjoyment to your diet, as long as they're properly prepared, eaten in moderation, not refined (soon to be explained) and organic (many grains are heavily sprayed and genetically modified).

That's not to say there aren't drawbacks. In fact, avoiding the complimentary bread basket served before most meals is recommended. Why? The body treats refined grains like sugar, upsetting your blood-sugar balance and contributing to weight gain and insulin resistance. In addition, unless grains are soaked or sprouted, their bran layer will contain phytic acid, which reduces mineral absorption and acts as an enzyme inhibitor, which interferes with digestion. And, overall, grains cause the body to produce mucus.

Grains are refined when their bran and germ layers are removed. They are further refined when they're milled into flour for breads and pasta. In fact, white wheat flour is one of the worst of the refined grains. It has a high gluten content, few nutrients and it's usually adulterated with bleaching agents and other chemicals to enhance its performance. Unfortunately, refined wheat flour is used in a whopping 90 percent of baked goods. Additionally, flour is prone to rancidity, and it causes a big, unhealthy spike in blood sugar levels (because the fiber isn't there to slow down the release of glucose).

Preparation techniques make a big difference as well; traditional methods yield more-nutritious, easier-to-digest dishes. When possible, opt for sprouted grains. These have been soaked in water until germination occurs, thereby neutralizing the grain's phytic acid content and increasing the availability of its nutrients. You can now find sprouted breads at health-focused eateries.

Sourdough is another smart choice since it's naturally leavened with a traditional fermentation technique that offers the same benefits of sprouting and creates lactobacillus—a probiotic that aids digestion.

To sum up: Say yes to moderation, traditional preparation methods and whole grains— and no to refined, milled and non-organic versions. An overview of key grains follows. They are divided into gluten grains and non-gluten grains for people who are allergic or sensitive. Even if you aren't, cutting down on gluten may be good for your health.

GLUTEN GRAINS

WHEAT is highest in gluten of all the grains, which is why it's the universal choice for bread-making. Gluten helps bread to rise. It's also the main ingredient in most pasta, pizza crusts, pastries, crackers, cakes and cookies, and is even used as a thickener in sauces. Incidentally, seitan—a popular meat substitute for vegetarians and vegans—is essentially wheat gluten with the texture of meat, so go easy on it if you are concerned about gluten.

BULGUR AND COUSCOUS are hybrids of different wheat species. Used like rice, bulgur is a staple in Middle Eastern restaurants and is best known as the main ingredient in tabbouleh. Couscous is typically found in North African and Moroccan cuisine. Bulgur is a whole grain as the bran and germ are still intact; couscous is not.

KAMUT AND SPELT are naturally hybridized, ancient varieties of wheat. Kamut is actually the brand name for khorasan wheat. Because they have a different form of gluten than wheat, and are more nutritious, both make good substitutes. In fact, you may do well with spelt even if you're sensitive to gluten due to the difference in gluten composition. Health-focused eateries now offer spelt-based options.

RYE, rich in a variety of nutrients, is used in place of wheat in items like rye bread and German pumpernickel. Many delis, diners and sandwich shops offer rye or pumpernickel options.

BARLEY is one of the most ancient cultivated grains and is said to be soothing to the intestines. Typically restaurants will use pearled barley to make risotto. Opt for hulled barley when possible, as it is the most whole form.

NON-GLUTEN GRAINS

RICE is one of the richest sources of B vitamins and is served at all types of restaurants. As discussed above, brown rice is a more whole option. Black and wild rice are also good choices.

CORN today often comes from genetically modified crops, so always ask if it is organic. Many Mexican establishments use corn flour as the base for tortillas and arepas.

OATS stabilize blood sugar, reduce cholesterol, and soothe the intestines and nervous system. Not usually encountered at dinner, oat-based dishes like oatmeal, granola and muesli are common breakfast offerings. Oats also appear in some baked goods. Opt for steel-cut oats when possible, as they are the most whole form. Many restaurant chains are now incorporating steel-cut oats in their breakfast menus. Some oats may be processed with gluten. Be sure to check that the label says "gluten-free."

BUCKWHEAT is one of only a few commercial crops not routinely sprayed with pesticides, because it has its own natural resistance. With the longest gut transit time of all the grains, it is the most filling and stabilizing for blood sugar levels. Buckwheat flour is often used to make pancakes, and soba noodles at Japanese restaurants, while buckwheat groats, the most whole form, is often used in Russian cuisine (called kasha) and some granolas.

QUINOA, technically a seed, was a major staple for the Incas of South America. Its high protein content, mild taste and fluffy texture have made it enormously popular. Quinoa can now be spotted on menus across multiple cuisines.

AMARANTH is not as widely available in restaurants as other grains, but it is becoming increasingly popular due to its nutrition profile. Amaranth contains unique essential amino acids such as lysine, which is important for maintaining bone, cholesterol and heart health.

MILLET is another excellent option. While perhaps best known as birdseed in the U.S., this cereal grass is popular in Asian and African cuisine. It is easily digested and very nutritious, with a high silica content for healthy skin and bones.

LEGUMES

They're the punch line of bad jokes, true, but beans—as well as peas and lentils—confer many health benefits. Known as legumes, or pulses, they lower cholesterol, control blood-sugar imbalances and regulate bowel functions. Low in fat (with the exception of soy beans), they're a good source of vegetarian protein, fiber and B vitamins. From a culinary perspective, herbs and spices marry well with the mild taste of legumes, which absorb the flavor of sauces and have a pleasant texture that adds bulk to any meal.

For a few susceptible individuals, abdominal gas and bloating result from eating beans, no matter how carefully they are prepared. But most of us need not avoid beans for fear of their antisocial effects. A good chef knows that most varieties of beans should be presoaked, rinsed and thoroughly cooked to break down their indigestible sugars and destroy their enzyme inhibitors (if they haven't come from a can).

Here's the dish on beans:

CHICKPEAS, BLACK BEANS, KIDNEY BEANS, ADZUKI BEANS AND LENTILS crop up in numerous cultures, where they have nourished humankind for millennia. Chickpeas, also called garbanzo beans, are used to make the hummus and falafels of Mediterranean cuisine and are popular in Indian curries; black beans are used in Mexican burritos; kidney beans are the legume of choice for chili; the adzuki bean is popular in macrobiotic restaurants; and red lentils often form the basis of dhal (dal, daal, dahl), an easily digested Indian puree.

SOY BEANS merit a lengthier discussion because they're eaten so frequently and used in so many ways—and, in particular, associated with numerous health claims and controversies.

Asians have been including soy foods in their diets for thousands of years, a fact that's often touted as the main reason for Asians' longevity and low rates of certain cancers and other Western diseases. However, this may have more to do with the paucity of dairy and meat in the Asian diet, as well as the emphasis on vegetables and various lifestyle factors. The truth is that soy has never been eaten in large quantities in Asia. Note the miso soup in Japanese restaurants, in which only a few cubes of tofu float around. And the next time you order Chinese vegetables with soy-bean curd, observe how the vegetables and rice predominate. This marginal role for soy stands in stark contrast to the modern soy burger at the center of the vegetarian entrée. Over the past few decades, vegetarians and vegans in particular have become over-reliant on soy because it is a balanced protein and can be formed into mock meat products.

However, studies detailing soy's high nutrient content and positive effects have recently been contested by additional research. Soy is known to block the absorption of some nutrients and is thought to increase the likelihood of ovarian and breast cancer.

One solution is simply to cut back. Another is to be mindful of the kinds of soy products you consume. Organic, non-GMO soy is your best bet, as are soy products like miso, soy yogurt, natto and tempeh, all of which undergo a fermentation process in which otherwise non-viable nutrients are partly predigested—and phytates and enzyme inhibitors that cause gastric distress are neutralized. In addition, these forms of soy are endowed with probiotics. With the possible exception of soy yogurt, these healthy forms of soy are usually available in Chinese, Japanese and macrobiotic restaurants.

Tofu, perhaps the most ubiquitous form of soy in restaurants, provides some nutrition but should be eaten in moderation since it hasn't undergone the all-important fermentation process.

As for edamame, it's a whole food but not easy to digest—good for you, but not in excess.

Soy milk, soy ice cream and soy cheese, however, are highly processed and not fermented—best consumed only on occasion. They usually come with additives of one kind or another in an attempt to mimic the flavor and texture of the real thing.

TVP (textured vegetable or soy protein), which in similar forms goes by the names protein soy isolate or hydrolyzed plant (or soy) protein, should be completely avoided whenever possible. It is made from soybean meal after the oil has been processed out with chemicals and intense pressure. These soy products are typically used in veggie burgers and fake meat products. They bear a close chemical resemblance to plastic and may contain residues from processing, including petroleum solvents, sulfuric acids, hydrochloric acid and caustic soda. Those are just a few good reasons to bypass that fake turkey sandwich in favor of the tempeh Reuben.

#4

If you choose to eat animal products, consume only (a) high-quality and sustainably raised animals (ideally pasture-raised and grass-fed, but at least hormone- and antibiotic-free); and do so (b) in moderation—meaning smaller portions with less frequency.

Meat still enjoys a reputation as being as all-American as the Wild West and cowboy boots. But self-improvement is an all-American quality, too, and to do that it's best to cut down on your intake of animal products, including meat, poultry, dairy and eggs. This does not mean you have to become vegetarian or vegan. Each individual should do what's best for his or her body.

Remember how proponents of *The China Study* argue that meat eating is a leading cause of human disease, while followers of the nutritionist Weston A. Price say it is beneficial? That's not the only area of contention regarding animal products.

Another is whether animal fats cause heart disease. An increasingly vocal minority of researchers claim the cholesterol myth is just that—a myth. They believe that highly processed vegetable oils and hydrogenated fats are more artery-clogging and lead to more heart trouble than lard. Of course, adherents of veganism and vegetarianism eschew animal products for a variety of reasons, while others believe that those diets are lacking in essential nutrients such as vitamins B12 and D. Different people will side with different research; your genetic makeup or lifestyle may mean that eating meat is necessary for your body to function smoothly. To figure it out, experiment and think about how certain foods and dietary principles make you feel.

If you consume animal products, do so in moderation. Why? For one thing, eating too many provides more protein than necessary for human health, creating more acidity than the body can process and leading to problems like fatigue and osteoporosis. In addition, there's substantial evidence that the practice of raising animals for human consumption—especially in conventional corporate feedlots—is unsustainable and environmentally problematic. Easy ways to lower the percentage of animal products in your diet include thinking of meat as a side dish rather than a main course, as well as eating smaller portions and less frequently.

In addition, make sure that all the animal products you consume—beef, dairy, eggs, chicken and so on—come from high-quality, organic and pasture-fed animals. Animal products are a concentrated source of the medications, stress, hormones and environmental toxins that the animal has been exposed to. This is a good reason to steer clear of factory-farmed animals. Jammed together in pens where they never see sunlight and are injected with hormones and who knows what else, these animals are often very sick—part of the reason they're injected with excess antibiotics. That's a powerful argument for choosing an organic, pasture-fed animal, which won't have been subjected to stressful conditions or injected with toxins. Instead, it will have been raised similarly to the way it would have been in the wild. A pasture-raised cow, for instance, grazes on grass, gets exercise and is exposed to the sun, all of which results in a healthy cow—and extra benefits for us.

Please note, organic and grass-fed are not the same thing. While organic does ensure minimal to no use of excess hormones and antibiotics, they are still fed grains, corn or organic vegetarian feed. Often, this is for taste reasons, but sometimes, even these animals are purposefully overfed—a practice that makes them more desirable in the market but also more prone to disease. Since grass is the natural diet for most animals, animals that eat grains or corn—even if it's high-quality, organic—are not as healthy as their grass-fed counterparts and therefore not as healthy for humans.

THINK ABOUT IT: FACTORY-FARMED COWS AND OBESITY

To make more money, growth hormones are injected into factory-farmed animals, so each animal's cells contain these hormones. When we consume meat, we are eating the cells of the animal—and the growth hormones contained therein. Perhaps that's one of the reasons we are facing an epidemic of obesity?

COOKING METHODS MATTER

In addition to knowing where your animal products have come from, it is also important to prepare them properly. For instance, grilled or roasted meats are better for you than deep-fried dishes. Be aware, though: Meats smoked or barbecued on charcoal grills can develop a carcinogen called polycyclic aromatic hydrocarbons. Like most other foods, meat is best for your body when it has been cooked briefly and gently. Prolonged high heat reduces the amount of vitamins and minerals in meat and denatures its protein. Worse, it increases the toxicity of contaminants already there, such as nitrates and pesticides. Of course, with so many disease-causing pathogens showing up in animal products, it may not be such a bad idea to avoid rare or raw meat (which otherwise would be the healthiest way to consume high-quality, properly raised animal products).

However, when possible, ask that your meat not be overcooked. Medium-rare is a good option and usually what chefs prefer anyway.

REMINDER: DON'T NECESSARILY WORRY ABOUT ORGANIC CERTIFICATION

Small farmers who raise animals sustainably and without the use of antibiotics or hormones often can't afford to obtain the "certified organic" accreditation.

TIP: FOOD-COMBINING

Not all foods can be properly digested when eaten together. Concentrated starches and proteins, for instance, should be eaten separately, as protein causes the body to produce specific enzymes and hydrochloric acid, which increases the stomach's acidity. This makes it more difficult to digest starch.

Translation: Eating a lot of meat with starches like bread or potatoes can cause gas and indigestion. A food-combining solution: Pair heavy proteins like meat with vegetables, such as leafy greens, instead of with starches like breads, grains and potatoes.

To summarize: Make sure that the animal products you eat are high-quality and organic (that is, hormone- and antibiotic-free), and preferably grass-fed. In addition, consume them less often and in small portions—and eat them with vegetables (especially leafy greens) to counteract some of the potential negative effects. Order your meat medium-rare whenever possible. By making these tweaks to your diet, you ensure that high-quality meat, fish, poultry, dairy and eggs can become a healthy part of a balanced diet rather than a risk factor.

Here are details about the different types of meats you're likely to encounter on menus:

BEEF is a source of iron and vitamin B12, as well as essential fats. Cows raised in pastures—where they're exposed to the sun and eat grass—provide the healthiest meat; in fact, an anti-cancer nutrient called conjugated linoleic acid (CLA) occurs only in grass-fed animals.

CHICKEN, LAMB AND PORK, all sources of complete protein, can be good for you, like beef, if you choose an organic, naturally raised animal and eat it in moderation. When it comes to pork, though, don't be fooled by the advertising "The Other White Meat." It's probably less healthy for you than chicken or lamb. Above all, it makes such a difference to your health that we'll repeat: Order free-range, naturally fed chicken, lamb or pork—and consume small portions.

GAME ANIMALS like bison and venison are among the healthiest kinds of meats because most often they come from freshly killed animals that lived in the wild. These animals are leaner than beef and boast a higher proportion of omega-3 fatty acids. In addition, they're less likely to be contaminated or diseased. It is becoming easier to find bison and venison in trendy restaurants, as well as establishments emphasizing organic dishes, although, for some, venison's gamey flavor is an acquired taste.

CURED MEATS like sausages, luncheon meats and bacon can be OK in moderation; it all comes down to how they are raised and made. I recommend cutting out luncheon meats altogether—nearly all of them contain carcinogenic preservatives such as nitrates. But if you can't stay away from, say, bologna, at least opt for nitrate-free varieties. Two requirements should be met before you purchase bacon or sausage: (1) The meat should have come from a good-quality animal, and (2) the way the meat was made should be as natural as possible. Sausage without casings or fillers, produced on the premises at an organic restaurant, for instance, gets a thumbs-up—as long as you eat it in moderation.

FOIE GRAS AND VEAL tend to be served only in upscale restaurants. The former is the liver of a fattened-up goose or duck, and the latter is the meat of a milk-fed (or sometimes formula-fed) baby calf. A lot of people avoid veal and foie gras (French for "fat liver") for moral reasons. Since they don't provide any particular health benefits, it's best avoiding them altogether.

COLD-WATER FISH like salmon, mackerel, cod and sardines are

chock-full of heart-healthy omega-3 fatty acids as well as fat-soluble vitamins and minerals, including iodine. Unfortunately, these benefits are minimized if the fish is conventionally farm-raised, a technique that results in more PCBs, mercury and disease—and fewer omega-3s. Plus, the feed for farmed salmon usually contains dye to give the flesh a pink color.

If you want the benefits of organically farm-raised or wild fish, salmon is probably the easiest fish to find at restaurants. Most nutritious in its raw form (for instance, as sashimi), it's also healthy when steamed or baked. Skip tempura, though; it involves dipping the fish in batter before deep-frying in hot oil.

SCAVENGER FISH include tuna, swordfish, carp and catfish. They eat almost anything they find in the sea, including dead fish (yum!). That's why their tissues are likely to contain the toxins of other fish, like PCBs and mercury; it's also why scavenger fish are considered no-no's for women who are pregnant or breastfeeding. If you like fish, stick mostly to the cold-water kind.

SHELLFISH like scallops, clams, mussels, oysters, shrimp, crabs and lobsters should be eaten in moderation and only while very fresh and in season. Shellfish spoil easily and are a common cause of food poisoning, as well as being prone to contamination. Be sure yours are sourced from clean waters.

To help you make quality seafood choices while dining out, download the Monterey Bay Aquarium's Seafood Watch mobile app. It lists fish both high in omega-3 fatty acids and low in environmental contaminants.

DAIRY AND EGGS

MILK'S big selling point is that it's a source of calcium. Yet research shows that milk's acidity means it can actually leach calcium from our bones. In addition, milk's low magnesium content relative to its calcium content means our bodies may not be able to benefit from milk's calcium, as they are required to be in balance for proper utilization. Calcium is better obtained from vegetables, seeds and nuts. Many people are lactose intolerant; only a third of the world's population possesses the genetic mutation required for the proper digestion of dairy. Populations from Asian and African descent have an especially high percentage of milk-intolerant individuals, which is why you're not likely to find many dairy products on their menus.

This doesn't mean milk is the devil, at least not for people who digest it well—as long as you get it from grass-fed cows, or at minimum, opt for an organic version. Avoiding products containing Recombinant Bovine Growth Hormone (aka RBGH), a genetically engineered drug associated with growth abnormalities and malignant tumors, is recommended. Another reason to go organic: Dairy cows fed unnatural diets, forced to produce excessive quantities of milk, and confined to small stalls or kept in unhygienic conditions often suffer from infected udders. This infection, called mastitis, causes the sick cows to release pus into their milk.

CHEESE can be enjoyed as part of a wholesome meal so long as it is from an organic, grass-fed source. Raw cheeses tend to preserve the most nutrients. Sheep and goat cheeses are another smart alternative. They are easier to digest than cheese made from cow's milk. These cheeses are increasingly popular in restaurants, where you might find them atop salads and as sandwich fillings. Avoid processed cheese, a staple in sandwich shops, delis, and fast-food entrées; they usually contain additives such as emulsifiers, extenders, phosphates and hydrogenated oils. You'll likely find them easy to give up, considering their bland taste and plastic texture.

CULTURED DAIRY PRODUCTS like kefir, yogurt and sour cream are easier to digest than other dairy items because their lactose and casein are already partially broken down. Kefir (a fermented yogurt drink) and yogurt also supply some healthy gut-promoting probiotics.

BUTTER most often appears at your table accompanying that insidious complimentary breadbasket. Unless you have a dairy allergy, a moderate amount of butter—especially organic, from grass-fed cows— offers some benefits, including easily digested fats and the fat-soluble vitamins A and D.

EGGS are rich in vitamins, minerals and protein, and can be quite nourishing. Their cholesterol content, however, causes debate. When overcooked, the yolk becomes oxidized, meaning it transforms from a useful nutrient into a potentially harmful chemical. For that reason, avoid powdered eggs, which have been through a heating and drying process and therefore contain oxidized cholesterol. To avoid oxidation, order lightly poached or sunny-side-up eggs rather than scrambled or fried; similarly, soft-boiled trumps hard-boiled. Raw eggs are even more beneficial than the lightly cooked kind, although people susceptible to salmonella, such as the elderly, the infirm or pregnant women, should avoid them.

TIP: EAT THE WHOLE EGG

The yolk contains a good deal of nutrients the white doesn't provide, like anti-inflammatory choline and antioxidant lutein. Plus, the yolk promotes a healthy HDL/LDL cholesterol ratio. So eat the whole shebang, yolk and white. Your body will thank you.

As with dairy and meat, a chef's choice of egg supplier has implications for both nutritional quality and taste. Battery-caged hens are more likely to turn out eggs with salmonella, fewer nutrients and a bland or fishy taste—and the cruelty of crowding hens together is another reason to skip ordering such eggs. Free-range, pasture-raised hens, on the other hand, produce eggs with richer flavor and increased nutrient content. At the very least, stick with hormone- and antibiotic-free eggs taken from cage-free hens.

5

To feel better immediately, simply reduce your intake of artificial, chemical-laden processed foods as well as refined sugar and poor-quality oils.

THIS SECTION IS all about the food that makes your mouth water: sweeteners, seasonings, fats and oils, and beverages. While generally thought of as harmful, they don't have to be, as long as you approach these full-of-flavor foods the right way.

FATS AND OILS

They've got a less-than-savory rep, but don't be afraid of fats and oils. They play an important role in the human diet.

Fats slow the release of sugar from other foods, create a feeling of satisfaction, give us a source of energy, and allow us to absorb fat-soluble vitamins A, D, E and K by carrying them across the gut wall. In addition, our bodies use fats as building materials, incorporating them into cell membranes to create the right balance between firmness and flexibility.

We like to preach about its evils—weight gain, heart disease—while still associating fatty food with comfort and fun. The truth is, it can get complicated, so let's simplify. The list of different fats and oils is a long one, so here's what you need to know about the ones you are most likely to encounter at a restaurant.

TRANS FATS or hydrogenated oils, made by injecting hydrogen into liquid vegetable oils to make them more solid, should be completely avoided as they are probably the most harmful ingredient in our food supply. In fact, Los Angeles has ensured you'll avoid these oils because the city has banned the use of trans fats in restaurants, so it is far less likely than before that dining out will mean consuming damaged vegetable oils in the form of vegetable shortening and hydrogenated margarine.

VEGETABLE OILS like soybean and canola are the most commonly used cooking and frying oils and should be avoided as much as possible as they are usually made from GMO crops, are highly processed and lead to inflammation and a host of other ailments.

COCONUT OIL provides a unique medium chained fat that is easily burned for energy instead of stored in the body. It is also a source of lauric acid, which has anti-bacterial and anti-viral properties. More and more restaurants are now using coconut oil to prepare foods thanks to its ability to withstand higher temperatures and the many health benefits it provides. Try coconut meat as well—juice bars will often offer both coconut meat and oil as add-ins for smoothies.

HEMPSEED AND FLAXSEED are valued for their essential fatty acids, but they are best used whole and raw, since processing, storage and heating can turn these delicate oils rancid. They contain high levels of omega-3 (minus contaminants such as mercury and PCBs). It's best to eat the seeds ground. Hemp and flax oils are healthy only when cold-pressed; in that form they make excellent salad dressings. They are not suitable for cooking or baking.

THE PROS AND CONS OF FLAX

Flaxseed is known for being an excellent vegetarian source not only of omega-3 fatty acids but also of calcium, iron and vitamin E. However, the type of omega-3s flax provides is not the same as the type fish provides. That's why, if you're not a vegetarian, it's best to incorporate wild or organically farmed fish into your diet in addition to flaxseed.

TIP: THE BEST OILS FOR
COOKING

Most restaurants use
inflammatory refined
vegetable oils for cooking.
Well-sourced ghee, lard and
coconut oil are fats stable
enough to withstand higher
temperatures without too
many free radicals being
formed in the process. Ask
your restaurant what they
use for cooking.

OLIVE OIL is a monounsaturated fat. Even though it has negligible amounts of essential fatty acids, it's better than many other oils as it provides a good source of oleic acid, which can help stabilize blood sugar levels. To receive the most benefits, opt for extra-virgin, cold-pressed, organic olive oil and consume unheated when possible—for example, as a salad dressing or drizzled over veggies.

BUTTER has become cool again after the downfall of margarine because of its dangerous levels of trans fats (hydrogenated oils). As explained above, butter—especially organic butter from a grass-fed cow—has some health benefits when consumed in moderation. Margarine, on the other hand, can damage your arteries more than any amount of butterfat because of its aforementioned trans fats. Its overuse in recent years—along with oils like soy, sunflower and corn—has contributed to a national over-consumption of omega-6 fatty acids, a situation that has been linked to numerous health problems.

GHEE is a clarified butter—meaning the milk solids have been removed, so even those who are lactose intolerant may be able to digest it.

SALT AND SEASONINGS

Salt is our main source of sodium, an important mineral involved in many bodily processes. Our bodies rely on a balanced ratio of potassium (a mineral found mainly in fresh fruits and veggies) and sodium for the smooth functioning of our muscles, lungs, heart and nervous system, as well as for the water balance within our bodies. Most people get way more than enough sodium, as it is overabundant in our modern, processed meals—even restaurants tend to use too much. We need about one teaspoon of sodium per day, but many of us are consuming many times that amount. Potassium, however, is lacking because we don't eat enough fresh fruits and vegetables. Too much sodium can lead to raised blood pressure, muscle cramps and water retention.

Next time you dine out, request that your meal be prepared with less salt. You'll be amazed at how quickly you lose the desire for excess salt and start to find too much unappealing.

TIP: GOOD SALT SUBSTITUTES

One clever and healthful way to reduce your sodium intake at a restaurant is to ask for herbs or spices to be substituted instead, a move that will increase the flavor of your meal while adding health benefits. Some of the best additions are garlic, a natural antibiotic; ginger, which prevents against nausea; cayenne, a circulation enhancer; turmeric, an anti-inflammatory; and green herbs such as parsley or cilantro, good sources of vitamins and chlorophyll.

REFINED TABLE SALT tends to be processed and altered with chemicals—it's sodium chloride with no nutritional benefits. Delete it from your diet, since it contributes to the sodium-potassium imbalance described above and usually contains aluminum to boot.

KOSHER SALT is a coarse salt with no additives; its thick crystal grains help to cure meat and are used in the process of making meat kosher—thus its name. Foodies like this salt for its texture and taste. Perhaps because it appears in gourmet foods, it's sometimes thought to be healthier than table salt. That's not the case, however; there's no nutritional difference between table and kosher salt. The latter may be marginally more healthful because it doesn't have additives, but don't be fooled into thinking it's good for you.

SEA SALT OR HIMALAYAN CRYSTAL SALT both appear at some restaurants and are fine to eat in moderation. Natural and unprocessed, they contain minerals, have a better flavor than table salt and tend to be prized by top chefs. Although sea and crystal salt are gaining in popularity, they're still most likely to crop up only in the kitchens of health-food or gourmet restaurants. At raw-food restaurants, they're usually the only kind of salt offered.

SHOYU AND TAMARI, both commonly referred to as soy sauce, are more or less interchangeable; both are fermented soy condiments, except that tamari is wheat-free. Asian and health-food restaurants serve shoyu and tamari, where they're sometimes also used for stir-frying. Health-conscious diners prefer naturally brewed versions over highly processed and additive-laden cheaper imitations. However, soy sauce is a questionable substitute for table salt because of the soy, wheat and inevitable processing. Unless stated on the label, soy sauce is not a low-sodium alternative and is best used sparingly.

SWEETENERS

"You're sweet." "How sweet it is." "That's sweet." The English language is peppered with remarks about how sweet sweetness is. So it's understandable that sugary foods tend to illicit the most resistance and guilt from people.

It's not exactly a news flash that refined white sugar and the more insidious high-fructose corn syrup are bad for us. It's difficult to get away from, though, because sugar is in all kinds of foods—not just bottled drinks and desserts, but also packaged foods and savory sauces.

Even if we're aware of which foods contain refined white sugar, it's hard not to order them. That's because sugar is biologically and emotionally addictive. Stop eating it and you may experience withdrawal symptoms. Eat some and you will crave more. Consider how children are offered sweets if they're "good" or "behave." To make matters worse, it seems that we have been biologically programmed to seek out sweetness as a way to avoid poison, which tends to be bitter. But it's a safe bet that evolution intended for us to eat fruits rather than doughnuts.

Even though you know that sweets aren't good for you, it's worth pointing out the many ways they're bad. Sugar is an anti-nutrient, not only giving the body zero nutrition but actually robbing us of goodies. Plus, it's probably the major contributor to weight gain. At a certain point of saturation the body converts it to fat, putting excess sugar into storage in order to quickly remove it from the blood where it would otherwise create havoc. After all, there is only so much sugar that we can use as energy. Sugar has been linked to a variety of other ailments, from lowered immunity and poor gut flora to cancer and diabetes. Yet research at George Washington University shows that the average American consumes 30 teaspoons of sugar and sweeteners per day!

So what should we do? We have to be smart about our approach to sugar. Once you begin to take better care of yourself in other areas of your life and eat better-quality foods, your sugar cravings tend to lessen. Sometimes exercise helps, as does eating a bit more protein and drinking more water. And consider switching to more natural, gentler forms of sweeteners. Take these steps and over time you will gradually find that refined sugar actually tastes too sweet. True, it may take a while, but this approach can really work, even for the most avid sugar addict.

Let's take a look at some of the common sweeteners you will encounter at restaurants:

WHITE TABLE SUGAR, HIGH-FRUCTOSE CORN SYRUP AND EVEN BROWN SUGAR should be avoided as much as possible.

ORGANIC RAW CANE SUGAR, FLORIDA CRYSTALS AND TURBINADO SUGAR have gained in popularity and are commonly found on the tables and in desserts at health-food restaurants. These sugars are a slightly better option than the completely refined stuff since they retain some nutrients and are better for the environment, but they're not healthy.

MAPLE SYRUP AND BROWN RICE SYRUP are preferable to all the above. They are the most commonly consumed natural sweeteners. They are OK in moderation if they are pure and of a high quality. Maple syrup is a better option because it has a lower glycemic index and provides more minerals. (Please note: Aunt Jemima is not real maple syrup!)

RAW HONEY is a far better choice than many of the other sweeteners, as it is rich in antioxidants, enzymes and various healing co-factors.

RAW AGAVE NECTAR has its issues, including a very high fructose content and the likelihood of poor production quality. Use it in moderation from an organic source.

COCONUT PALM SUGAR is becoming a popular choice due to its low impact on blood sugar levels and its ability to retain minerals and phytonutrients during processing. It is still a sugar, though, so like all sweeteners it should be consumed in moderation.

STEVIA, extracted from the sweet leaves of the stevia plant, is also becoming increasingly popular for its sugary taste and safeness for diabetics, although some people are not crazy about its aftertaste. In addition, there is conflicting research regarding its safety.

ARTIFICIAL SWEETENERS like Splenda, Equal and NutraSweet (aspartame) should be avoided as there are many adverse reactions reported to the FDA. Plus, there is convincing evidence that these artificial sweeteners can still mess with insulin levels thus leading to weight gain.

BEVERAGES

A sparkling stream of water runs through a picturesque valley. This could be an ad for anything from beer to an energy drink. The point? Advertisers know that we know that water is good for us. So they use it to sell beverages that aren't so good. Read on for details about the drinks you'll find at restaurants.

WATER should be your beverage of choice, as it's the most natural and purest liquid you can get. In restaurants, bottled water tends to be overpriced, but it may be worth it if the only other option is tap water, which may be polluted by contaminants. Filtered tap water is the best option; it's free, safe and better for the environment than bottled water (plus, you avoid ingesting chemicals that may leach into the water from the plastic bottle). If the restaurant's water is filtered, the food that's cooked in it will be safer for you as well.

FRUIT JUICES are OK to drink but quite sugary and usually void of fiber. Try diluting them with water.

VEGETABLE JUICES are a better option. They count toward your nutrient intake, especially with dark greens thrown in.

SODAS AND SOFT DRINKS are composed of unfiltered, artificially carbonated water with added sugar (or, worse, corn syrup or artificial sweeteners), flavorings, colorings, preservatives and sometimes caffeine. In addition, their high phosphoric-acid content is associated with osteoporosis. Not a recipe for health. Avoid them altogether, especially the diet ones, which are loaded with artificial sweeteners that, research has suggested, actually may cause weight gain.

COFFEE can provide a much-needed lift. Still, it's best to reduce caffeine consumption. Sure, coffee beans may contain antioxidants; plus, some people metabolize caffeine better than others. However, caffeine in general, and coffee in particular, is linked to raised blood pressure, insomnia, nervous conditions, osteoporosis and certain

TIP: WATER TEMPERATURE

Room-temperature water is the healthiest kind. That's because cold water is difficult to digest, so ask for yours with no ice—but with a slice of lemon, which makes the water more alkalizing and cleansing.

TIP: ELECTROLYTES FOR ATHLETES

Looking to replenish those electrolytes after a tough workout? Replace your Gatorade with coconut water. It's loaded with electrolytes and a naturally sweet taste.

cancers. At the very least, drinking caffeine with your meal reduces the availability of minerals in the food—it leaches them out.

If you can't resist ordering a cup, check whether the restaurant offers an organic, fair-trade or shade-grown version.

TIP: COFFEE REPLACEMENT

Raw cacao beans, or nibs, make a tasty interim crutch for people trying to break their coffee habit. Cacao will give you a lift, partially from caffeine and partially from other natural, happiness-inducing chemicals. Plus, they are extraordinarily rich in magnesium and antioxidants. (Sorry, chocolate bars with their cooked cacao and sugar don't count as a whole-food alternative to coffee.) Some macrobiotic and health-focused restaurants will offer a grain coffee substitute, typically made from chicory. They are caffeine-free yet have coffee's robust taste.

GREEN TEA may be the most healthful, or at least the most benign, of all caffeinated beverages. That's because it contains polyphenols, a type of antioxidant that can reduce blood pressure (coffee's opposite effect), lower blood fats and combat those free radicals we encounter in a city environment. It contains much less caffeine than coffee. In addition, it has theanine, which mitigates some of caffeine's effects to produce a calmer type of energy and prevents a caffeine "hangover."

BLACK TEA has fewer antioxidants and more caffeine than green. But it doesn't contain as much caffeine as coffee unless it is steeped for an especially long time.

Both green and black teas come from the same plant, often one that's been heavily sprayed, so seek an organic version.

HERBAL TEAS may be the best hot drink overall, since they are naturally caffeine-free and boast mild therapeutic benefits. For instance, peppermint and ginger tea both are helpful to drink after a heavy meal, since they aid digestion; chamomile, as you probably know, has calming properties.

DECAFFEINATED COFFEE OR TEA is fine to drink if the caffeine has been removed using the Swiss-water process. Otherwise, residue from chemicals used to remove the caffeine might remain—a non-issue if the product is certified organic. And note that all decaffeinated beverages still contain some traces of caffeine.

FERMENTED DRINKS like amazake (made from rice), kefir (a lacto-fermented yogurt drink), traditional ginger ale, apple cider and kombucha (a fermented tea drink), are mostly found in health-focused restaurants. It may take a few tries to become accustomed to their tangy taste, but they are worth getting used to, as they are rich in enzymes and probiotics and aid in strong digestion.

WINE is fermented, true, but its alcohol content tends to neutralize the much-touted health benefits. Although some research may say that wine is good for you in various small ways, some people use that as an excuse to drink too much. Even in relatively small amounts, wine is an anti-nutrient, particularly good at robbing the body of B vitamins. All alcohol can make you accident prone, dehydrated, unable to concentrate and even aggressive. It should be avoided if you are susceptible to candida overgrowth. And it's worth repeating: Long-term drinking to excess, whether labeled alcoholism or not, can result in liver damage and stomach ulcers, not to mention a host of social and emotional problems.

Still, like coffee, alcohol can be useful in moderation. After a stressful day at work, a relaxing glass of wine can make all the difference to your enjoyment of a meal and your ability to converse with fellow diners. Plus, it can stimulate the digestive process. Red wine in particular provides some antioxidant benefits and is said to be good for the heart in moderate amounts. As with coffee, though, there is no need to rely on wine for your antioxidants; think vegetables and fruits instead. Opt for organic and/or biodynamic wines when possible as they are free of pesticides and the producers usually go to extraordinary lengths to create special, pure growing conditions. Also look for sulfite-free or NSA wines, meaning "no sulfites added." Sulfites occur naturally in grapes, but many vineyards add more to prevent bacterial growth, oxidation and a vinegary taste. Many people experience allergic side effects, including headaches, when they consume sulfites, and some connoisseurs prefer the taste of a low-sulfite wine. White wine generally has fewer sulfites than red.

BEER, ALE AND LAGER are lower in alcohol than wine, but it's still important to watch the amount you drink. They also contain gluten, which can be problematic to those with sensitivities.

HARD LIQUOR OR SPIRITS such as vodka, tequila, and rum are much higher in alcohol than both wine and beer, which is why they're often diluted with tonic water or fruit juice. Be especially careful of these because of the high alcohol content.

TIPS FOR DINING OUT

NOW YOU HAVE an idea of some of the best foods to pick while dining out. How do you put these ideas into practice? First, remember the Five Keys to Clean Eating:

1 There's more than one right way to eat.
2 The overwhelming majority of your diet should consist of natural, high-quality and whole foods.
3 Everyone would be better off if a larger proportion of their diet consisted of plants—mostly vegetables (in particular, leafy greens), and some nuts, seeds and fruits.
4 If you choose to eat animal products, consume only (a) high-quality and sustainably raised animals (ideally pasture-raised and grass-fed, but at least hormone- and antibiotic-free), and do so (b) in moderation—meaning smaller portions with less frequency.
5 To feel better immediately, reduce your intake of artificial, chemical-laden processed foods as well as sugar, caffeine and alcohol.

We want to make it easy for you to transition—and stick—to healthier dining, so here are several psychological and social tips for following what's outlined above.

THE RIGHT APPROACH

MOTIVATION

This is the why: You've got to know why you're doing something to do it successfully. So, why are you changing your diet? We all want to be slimmer, trimmer, better looking. And those are OK reasons. But there are better reasons, like heightened energy, greater strength, fewer illnesses and clearer thinking. It helps to get excited about getting the most out of life and bringing enjoyment not only to yourself but also to other people—not to mention planet Earth— since our food choices have a major impact on the environment.

So, right now, take out a sheet of paper and write down why you want to eat healthier. Once you've written down your motivations, commit to them—that is, set a clear intention. It's a great launching pad for getting—and staying—motivated.

The other part of intention and motivation? Believing that, yes, you can do this. Don't simply hope you can succeed; know that you will.

AWARENESS

Awareness means (a) remembering your motivation (your why) and intention (your commitment); and (b) being aware of the various forces that might act against you. Admitting that challenges exist is a necessary step to moving beyond them. These challenges may include things like physical cravings and addictions, emotional attachments to food, cultural conditioning, advertising and a lack of education about healthy eating. Peer pressure is another biggie; you're going to need to keep your resolve if others try to coax you back to your old ways. Be aware that change can make others uncomfortable.

Awareness also means paying attention to how certain foods make you feel, physically and mentally. Keep a diet diary if that helps.

Begin to eliminate any foods or drinks that drain your energy, give you indigestion, make you irritable or create so much guilt when you consume them that you simply don't enjoy or digest them properly.

PATIENCE

Do you wish there was a magic formula for positive change? Actually, there is. Think of it as the magical trio: patience, perseverance and resilience. And yes, we know, these qualities aren't so simple.

In dietary terms, these words mean realizing that lasting improvements take time and application. At first you may need to be satisfied with eating healthier about half of the time, but once you do get to that 50/50 mark, you will have the momentum to go further, slowly, going from 60/40 to 70/30 and onward, until you may even hit 90/10. Don't be too extreme right away, though.

YOUR CHOICES AS AN INDIVIDUAL

Part of being human is having the ability to make conscious choices based on our intentions and what is best for us. Just start with the 50 percent rule and see what happens. En route, don't be discouraged by slip-ups. Notice them and move on. Try not to be too rigid with yourself or others. People who are hard on themselves tend to be judgmental of others. That's counterproductive. If your mission to eat better becomes a strict chore and strains your relationships, it will make you miserable and you will long for your old, comfortable ways. Remember, what works for your body may not necessarily work for someone else's; that's bio-individuality.

HOW TO EAT

STAY NOURISHED: Stay on top of cravings by beginning the day with a sustaining breakfast and a nutritious lunch. Make lunch your largest meal of the day, and when possible eat a fairly light dinner early—a large salad or vegetarian option, for instance—so you're not overeating close to bedtime. And keep hydrated all day by drinking water.

CHEW: It seems obvious, but you'd be surprised how many people don't, at least not properly. Thorough mastication helps your body digest nutrients better. To see just how little chewing we all do, try chewing 10 to 20 times per mouthful or until the food becomes liquid—not easy, right?

EAT SLOWLY: Pause between bites to savor the flavors and check in with your stomach to ask it "Are you full yet?" This will make your meal last longer and help to prevent the discomfort and weight gain associated with overeating.

DON'T OVEREAT: Eating slowly and chewing properly helps to prevent this, but note how much you order in the first place. Practice portion control. And realize that it's unnecessary to order an appetizer and dessert as well as an entrée. If you're still hungry after eating slowly, you can always order more. Have a light fruit snack before going out to eat; if you arrive at a restaurant starving, you're likely to overeat. And skip the bread at the beginning of the meal.

AVOID DISTRACTIONS: If you're not good at blocking out extraneous noise and distractions, you might want to eat in silence or alone occasionally. But given that most meals—especially in restaurants—are a fun, shared experience, try to dine with people who don't give you indigestion. Keep heated debates to a minimum so that you can chew and assimilate the food properly. Reading and television are also distracting.

DON'T EAT UNDER STRESS: Anxiety and anger shut down the digestive function as part of the "fight or flight" response. Eating under such circumstances can cause indigestion. At such times you will be tempted to go for comfort foods or to overeat to numb your feelings. If you do arrive stressed at a restaurant, take a few deep breaths and remember your intention.

PRACTICE GRATITUDE: Be thankful for your food and for all the people and forces that brought it to your table: the sun that shone down on it, the farmer who grew it and the waiter who delivered it. Taking a moment to give thanks will calm you and remind you of your connection to the whole. It will also enable you to feel grateful for real, healthy food and simple pleasures.

ENJOY: Whatever you choose to eat—even if you know it is not perfectly healthy—allow yourself to enjoy it. Guilt is a stressor that makes you and your digestive system unhappy.

EXPERIMENT: It's that bio-individuality thing again. Experiment with different dietary theories and foods so that over time you can discover what works best for you and your body. At the very least, eat a few meals each week with no animal products by ordering proteins such as beans. Whatever you do, eat your veggies!

SOCIAL SITUATIONS

Even with the best intentions you will occasionally end up at a restaurant that does not serve healthy food or with a group of diners who do not share your dietary goals.

What to do?

ORDER SIDES: Most restaurants have a selection of side dishes from which you can create a meal.

SPECIAL ORDER: An accommodating, creative chef will be happy to make something especially for you. Try requests like: "I know it's not on the menu, but could you put together a plate of vegetables and beans for me?" or "I'd like an extra-large version of your side salad as my entrée."

SKIP THE FREEBIES: Just because the bread is complimentary does not mean that you have to eat it. Likewise, try to ignore those fortune cookies or mints that arrive with the bill.

ASK FOR SAUCE ON THE SIDE: If the salad dressings and sauces are not up to par, ask the server to bring them on the side so you can monitor how much you use.

ASK FOR SUBSTITUTIONS: Some restaurants charge for doing this, and some don't. In any case, it is worth asking for things like green veggies or even baked potatoes instead of french fries.

WHAT TO ASK

When the cooking is out of your control, it's hard to know exactly what you're about to consume and where it has come from. Here are some illuminating questions to ask your server.

How was this prepared?

Some establishments make meals from scratch, while others pre-make recipes in bulk and microwave them on demand, or plate veggies and fruits straight from the can. By asking your server how your dish has been prepared (Was it sautéed? Boiled? Steamed?) you can gather a bit more information for peace of mind.

Can I substitute?

Always see if you can swap for a more whole option. For example, see if you can get brown rice in place of white.

Where was this sourced from? Is it organic?

It may feel awkward at first, but getting into the habit of questioning your server about whether your chicken is organic or your hamburger is from a grass-fed source is an important way of ensuring you aren't consuming added hormones or antibiotics.

Want to know if your veggies have been sautéed in a low-quality oil? If your cake has been made with margarine? Your servers are meant to be a resource. Use them!

Routinely asking these questions is a great way to build your "food radar"—a muscle of sorts that will grow stronger with use. The more you check for the differences between whole and unwholesome, high-quality and run-of-the-mill, real and processed, the more automatic eating real, whole and high-quality foods will become.

Hopefully you now have enough inspiration, motivation and information to put the Five Keys to Clean Eating into action. It's time to start enjoying your food more than ever while getting healthier at the same time. You can have your naturally sweetened dessert and eat it, too!

So now let's get to the best part (we have a feeling you may have taken a peek already) and check out the restaurants.

THE CLEAN PLATES 100 LA

Clean Meats
The majority of meats served are, at a minimum, antibiotic- and hormone-free

Clean Fish
The majority of seafood served is from sustainable fisheries

Vegetarian-Friendly
A vegetarian can happily dine here

Clean Desserts
Emphasis on organic ingredients and natural sweeteners

Gluten-Free-Friendly
Those with gluten sensitivities can happily dine here

Grab-and-Go
Online ordering available for pick-up and/or fast food options

Delivers

$15 and Under
Meal for one

$15–$30

$30–$60

$60 and Up

THE TOP FIVES

A round-up of our top picks for specific dietary wants and needs.

BRUNCH

Flore Vegan p. 103
Huckleberry p. 113
Sqirl p. 154
Square One Dining p. 155
Tavern p. 159

VEGETARIAN/VEGAN

Cafe Gratitude p. 80
Crossroads Kitchen p. 91
Gracias Madre p. 109
Powerplant Superfood Cafe p. 144
Sage p. 149

FLEXITARIAN

*(Accommodates vegetarians, meat-eaters
and those with gluten sensitivities)*

Akasha p. 68
Cooks County p. 88
Lyfe Kitchen p. 126
MB Post p. 129
Tar & Roses p. 158

GLUTEN-FREE

Artisan House p. 71
Azla p. 73
Elf Cafe p. 95
Evo Kitchen p. 97
M Café de Chaya p. 127

PALEO-FRIENDLY

Belcampo Meat Co. p. 174
Salt's Cure p. 150
Tavern p. 159
Tender Greens p. 160
Venice Ale House p. 163

ABIGAILE

1301 Manhattan Ave.
310-798-8227

abigailerestaurant.com
@abigaile

Cuisine:
American
(Contemporary)

Neighborhood:
Hermosa Beach

Meals Served:
Brunch, Dinner

With three dining rooms, three patios, an organic brewery and menu options for any palette, Abigaile is a local's hangout and a destination worth the drive. Executive chef Tin Vuong's globally influenced dishes are the largest small plates we've seen, and are generous indeed given the price point. Everything we ate was excellent, but the standouts included the foraged wild mushrooms with creamy polenta and the roasted medjool dates and kale salad.

Vuong's dedication to sustainability results in quality ingredients across the board. Vegan dishes include the Buddha Belly Feast of Bhutanese red rice, eggplant and tofu, which was exotically spiced and had the right amount of umami. Our "Carnage" choice, the crispy pork loin bi bim bap, provided a tasty spin on the trendy Korean dish. The main dining room has a punk rock vibe, but the staff is professional and polished. If you dine before sunset, bring sunglasses (and a hearty appetite).

CLEAN BITES

- Abigaile brews its own beer in-house!
- Some of the desserts are sweetened with maple syrup. Ask your server.

Cuisine:
American
(Contemporary)

Neighborhood:
Culver City

Meals Served:
Brunch, Lunch, Dinner

AKASHA

9543 Culver Blvd.
310-845-1700

akasharestaurant.com
@AkashaCC

A standout on the crowded Culver City foodie map, Akasha is a
neighborhood spot with special-occasion flair and destination-dining
appeal. While chef Akasha Richmond is a former personal chef to
celebs, the stars in this kitchen are unquestionably the carefully
sourced ingredients.

The menu names the local family farms that supply the restaurant's
produce for seasonal salads and vegetable sides, like a simply elegant
Schaner Farms lettuce salad studded with petite radishes and almonds
lightly dressed in avocado vinaigrette. Flexitarian alert: Big plates
range from vegetable quinoa pilaf and mushroom flatbread to wild king
salmon and New York steak. There's not always cohesion in Richmond's
imaginative compositions, but when her alchemy works, it's solid gold.

Come with a date to linger under the hushed lights in the wood-
paneled dining room or pop into the attached cafe for a quick sandwich
and Intelligentsia coffee.

CLEAN BITES

- Must try: If you spot the sausage flatbread with rapini, order it.
- Richmond was Michael Jackson's personal and concert tour chef.
- The restaurant works with Share Our Strength's No Kid Hungry
  campaign.
- Seafood is sourced from Marine Stewardship Council-certified
  fisheries.

AMMO

1155 N. Highland Ave.
323-871-2666

ammocafe.com
@ammorestaurant

Cuisine:
Californian

Neighborhood:
Hollywood

Meals Served:
Brunch, Lunch, Dinner

With its dim lighting, red banquettes, white tablecloths and California fare, Ammo appears at first glance to be a standard, upscale Hollywood haunt. But the slick setting is merely a polished veneer for a place that's a little bit country at heart.

The menu, largely sourced from local farms, is dictated by the seasons. Dishes are at their best when the kitchen lets the seasonal produce shine, like peak-of-ripeness heirloom tomatoes napped in a light vinaigrette and paired with a creamy, decadent burrata.

There's an Italian lilt to the menu, but we'd skip the pizzas and pastas for the entrées of healthy proteins and veggies. An absolute standout is the wild sea bass in a delicate white wine and fresh herb broth studded with baby carrots, cherry tomatoes and olives (or whatever's freshest at the market). We love that the food, not the scene, rules this corner of Hollywood.

CLEAN BITES

- Must try: wild sea bass entrée.
- Check out the restaurant's website to see the farms it collaborates with.
- Want to sample Ammo on the Westside? There is a limited menu at Ammo at the Hammer museum.

Cuisine:
French, Mediterranean

Neighborhood:
Beverly Grove

Meals Served:
Brunch, Lunch, Dinner

A.O.C.

8700 W. 3rd St.
310-859-9859

aocwinebar.com
@aocla

Chef Suzanne Goin and sommelier Caroline Styne, the duo behind Lucques (p. 125), have set the standard for small-plates eating in Los Angeles. A.O.C.'s communal bar table, tasteful dining room and picturesque patio buzz with the convivial, très European spirit of the good life: sharable, artfully composed farm-to-table dishes and global wines.

Goin's genius lies in her ability to develop a synergy of flavors while maintaining the integrity of each ingredient. Warm, parmesan-stuffed roasted dates are enrobed in smoky bacon; long-cooked cavolo nero retains its earthy essence. Salads balance lush fruits with crisp vegetables, and on the protein tip you're likely to find a market fish plate and flavorful hanger steak.

At dinner, there are also larger platters intended to be shared among four people, such as lamb tagine or wood-oven roasted lobster. But at lunch, individual plates and focaccia sandwiches are the focus. Private parties: Reserve the rustic wine room upstairs.

CLEAN BITES

- The wines are organic, sustainable and biodynamic.
- Goin has been honored by the Monterey Bay Aquarium for her dedication to sustainable seafood sourcing.

ARTISAN HOUSE

600 S. Main St.
213-622-6333

artisanhouse.net
@ArtisanHouseLA

Cuisine:
American
(Contemporary),
Mediterranean

Neighborhood:
Downtown

Meals Served:
Breakfast, Brunch,
Lunch, Dinner

The trendy industrial-modern vibe at Artisan House (24-foot-high ceilings, mercury-distressed mirrors, exposed brick and pipes) isn't just for show. Located in the historic Pacific Electric Building, the restaurant's decor reflects its legacy, including marble tabletops salvaged from the building's original floors.

The space blends old and modern, as does the California Mediterranean menu. Generously sized branzino is classically baked in parchment with lemon, while a lightly dressed truffle beet salad arrives with modernist cubes of feta, grapefruit and beets architecturally stacked. A spicy tuna tartare is anything but, although the sweet tuna is nicely complemented with pistachios and fresh herbs from the restaurant's rooftop garden.

Good for groups (there are several communal white oak tables), you'll find few who will object to the solid roster of California-casual stalwarts: artisanal pizzas with chewy, thin crusts, organic quinoa, fresh seafood pastas, and seared wild tuna or grass-fed beef tenderloin steaks.

CLEAN BITES

- The adjoining Artisan House marketplace has a to-go food counter and is filled with wine, vegan snacks and organic produce, plus a wall of beverages with everything from organic hemp milk to small-batch craft brews.
- Executive chef Jason Ryczek stocks the rooftop garden with fresh herbs, salad greens and a few specialty vegetables.

Cuisine:
Californian

Neighborhood:
Venice

Meals Served:
Brunch, Lunch, Dinner

AXE

1009 Abbot Kinney Blvd.   axerestaurant.com
310-664-9787

Axe (pronounced Ah-shay) takes its name from a Yoruba salutation that translates as "go with the power of the gods and goddesses." We suspect there is indeed something divine at work here, as the eclectic, seasonal fare is as soulful and scrumptious as it is sustainable.

The minimalist interior space is warmed by acacia wood accents and handmade jute lamps, while the garden patio attuned to the Venice breeze hosts a mesquite fire where grilled items such as escarole and fresh fish are prepared.

Our starter salad of shaved arugula was pure bliss, the spiciness of the greens offset by a salty hit of parmesan. Another highlight was the seared, sake-marinated filet of pasture-fed beef, which proved succulent and perfectly spiced with slivers of jalapeño. Special dieters, rejoice: Hearty veggie/brown rice bowls are served all day. The earthy fare is sure to nourish your body as well as your spirit.

CLEAN BITES

- The restaurant supports various foundations focused on fair food access and disaster relief.
- In addition to organic and seasonal produce, bulk staples such as grains, beans and oils are also purchased from organic distributors.
- Sustainable practices include composting, reverse-osmosis water filtration, and the use of biodegradable take-out containers and post-consumer waste paper products.

AZLA

3655 South Grand Ave.
213-745-7455

azlavegan.com
@azlavegan

Cuisine:
Ethiopian, Vegetarian/
Vegan

Neighborhood:
Historic South Central

Meals Served:
Lunch, Dinner

California vegan meets traditional Ethiopian cuisine at this quick-service, family-run stall in the multicultural Mercado la Paloma food court. It's billed as food "made with love," and with matriarch Azla Mekonen at the stoves, cooking with care, we believe it.

Flavorful Ethiopian wot (stews) are the heart of the operation. Gomen, a collard greens stew, gets a California update with the addition of kale. Another go-to is misir, a red lentil stew laced with berbere, a robust Ethiopian spice blend. Scoop up the stews with a spongy, tangy injera pancake—a gluten-free and nutrient-rich version made with quinoa and teff—or have yours served over brown rice.

An array of bright, seasonal salads add crunch and color to your combo plate. Both the keysir (marinated beets with quinoa) and shimbra (lemony kale with chickpeas) are fresh, light counterpoints to the spicy, filling stews.

Snag Ethiopian provisions and fashions in Azla's adjacent boutique.

CLEAN BITES

- Must try: nutrient-rich and gluten-free injera.
- Azla cooks only with olive oil.

Cuisine:
French

Neighborhood:
Highland Park

Meals Served:
Brunch, Lunch, Dinner

BA

5100 York Blvd.
323-739-6243

restaurantba.com

Artist and chef James Graham's Ba restaurant gives Highland Park some cachet. Graham's wife, Julia Latané, a sculptor, renovated their century-old storefront into a charming, cozy space.

We started with the mushroom brûlée, a rich custard of mushrooms topped with melted brie and baguette slices for dipping. But the salad with grilled peaches, heirloom tomato and burrata, lightly dressed with olive oil and basil, won our hearts; it was summer on a plate. The filet mignon was a succulent treat; the meat was tender and cooked beautifully. The wild Alaskan salmon was seared on the grill but moist inside. Both dishes came with piping hot roasted fingerlings and broccoli rabe.

However, the standout was the flourless chocolate cake; one of the best we've ever had. Graham sweetens it with molasses and honey and pairs it with baked cherries and fresh whipped cream. A typically cloying dessert was a revelation in his hands.

CLEAN BITES

- Get ready for an intimate experience—the dining room only seats 24 guests.
- Graham's interesting background includes time spent as an art student, caterer and pastry chef—and as a sous chef to Anthony Bourdain, with whom he worked at four New York restaurants.
- Check Ba's website to learn about its vendors.

BLOOM CAFE

5544 Pico Blvd.
323-934-6900

bloomcafe.com

Cuisine:
American (Casual)

Neighborhood:
Mid-City

Meals Served:
Breakfast, Lunch,
Dinner

Bright, modern, and eclectic, Bloom is the sort of casual cafe-cum-juice bar you wish you'd find in every neighborhood. The two-room, loft-like space is divided into a quick-service counter blending fresh fruit and veggie smoothies and a dining area dishing globally influenced healthy plates against a backdrop of rotating art and photography displays by local artists.

The lunch and dinner menu—an assortment of sandwiches, salads, burgers and bowls—hops the map from spice-trail Moroccan chicken to lemongrass-infused organic tofu curry. Vegans and vegetarians will relish animal-free soups and wraps, while meat lovers have plenty of health-oriented options, including a lean bison bolognese served over penne and burgers of grass-fed beef or free-range turkey (with the choice of a gluten-free bun to boot).

Perhaps the best part? Naturally sweetened, vegan and raw desserts!

CLEAN BITES

- Must try: the avocado/ahi tuna tartare tostada and the grilled salmon with mango bowl.
- Feel a cold coming on? Scoot over for one of Bloom's "cold zappers" with ginger, mint and rosemary.

BLUE COW KITCHEN & BAR

Cuisine:
American (Casual)

Neighborhood:
Downtown

Meals Served:
Lunch, Dinner

350 S. Grand Ave.
213-621-2249

bluecowkitchen.com
@bluecowkitchen

Blue Cow is the slightly more formal, sit-down sister restaurant to Mendocino Farms gourmet sandwich shop (p. 131), and since we're keen on their organic, artisanal approach to sandwich-making, we were thrilled to experience a wider menu.

Blue Cow's inventive sandwiches don't disappoint—the droves of office lunch breakers who migrate here from the surrounding high rise buildings for their gourmet sandwich fix are a testament to that. But we're equally excited by the salad, entrée and veggie side offerings, which change seasonally.

Take, for example, the scrumptious curried cauliflower, which pairs roasted cauliflower with Singaporean-style curry, garbanzo beans and curry pickles on house-made naan. It's a vegetarian dish good enough to make carnivores envious.

Meatier plates like roasted chicken, grilled salmon and braised short ribs come with a choice of hot or cold veggie side. With seasonal cocktails and craft beers, it's no wonder those lunch breakers return for happy hour.

CLEAN BITES

- Transparency is king here: Check out Blue Cow's website for a full list of farms it sources from.
- Special dieters at ease: The menu denotes dishes that are vegan and gluten-free or can be requested as such.
- The staff is super-knowledgeable about the menu.

BLUE HEN

1743 Colorado Blvd.
323-982-9900

eatatbluehen.com
@eatatbluehen

Cuisine:
Vietnamese

Neighborhood:
Eagle Rock

Meals Served:
Lunch, Dinner

Nestled in an Eagle Rock strip mall, Blue Hen might appear at first glance to be just another hole-in-the-wall noodle joint. Step inside, however, and you'll find an organic-friendly diamond in the rough.

Supporting local farms and organic practices is this Vietnamese kitchen's raison d'être. The offerings can be hit-or-miss—our order of fresh spring rolls was on the bland, limp side. But when they get things right, the dishes far exceed your typical strip-mall greasy spoon. The Vietnamese crepe stuffed with organic chicken, tofu or shrimp, along with onions and a plethora of bean sprouts, is one such accomplishment, as is the coconut-milk-rich, home-style curry with a side of crunchy, sautéed yu choy.

CLEAN BITES

- Must try: pho noodle soup—the broth is light with bold flavors instead of your typical greasy fare.
- Blue Hen serves organic tofu and dairy—a rarity for many Asian joints.
- Lots of spices and herbs are used in their cooking. Antioxidant boost!

Cuisine:
Italian

Neighborhood:
Culver City

Meals Served:
Brunch, Lunch, Dinner

BUCATO

3280 Helms Ave.
310-876-0286

bucato.la
@BucatoLA

Although Bucato is situated in the Helms Bakery complex, a bastion of progressive restaurants and design stores, the Italian gem manages to keep things "Old World." Cell phone use is politely discouraged, and chef Evan Funke (who previously cooked at Rustic Canyon [p. 148]) insists on a "no machine" policy for crafting the fresh pasta.

And oh, what a difference handmade makes. We swooned over the dense orecchiette, petite "ears" that served as tasty receptacles for a sugo of sausage, sprouting broccoli and a piquant dose of chili. The smallish portions mean you can enjoy the pasta without carb-overloading.

Veggies and proteins are equally well-executed. Sicilian-style cauliflower—flash fried and seasoned with melted anchovy, garlic, lemon zest and capers—is a must-order. Our flaky branzino paired deliciously with chunky eggplant caponata, and lamb chops with green garlic pesto were perfectly grilled and beautifully plated. You'll want to sneak a picture.

CLEAN BITES

- 70% of the restaurant is outdoors, so it accepts only same-day reservations. (Phone lines open daily at 9:30 a.m.)
- The staff personally visits the farms from which they source, to guarantee sustainable practices.
- The organic meats are butchered in-house!

CABBAGE PATCH

Multiple locations   cabbagepatchla.com
                          @eatcabbagepatch

Cuisine:
American (Casual)

Meals Served:
Lunch, Dinner

Cabbage Patch brings the garden to your bowl, offering a quick bite for those looking for an affordable and nutritious meal, while still utilizing organic, all-natural and locally sourced products.

The salads are simple and straightforward—all you have to do is pick your protein and add to any of Cabbage Patch's signature salad creations. We went with the French green lentil salad, which came with a generous portion of perfectly cooked lentils, mixed greens and avocado. The albacore tuna salad (with a free-range egg) was a bit bland on its own, but got a nice boost from the tangy lemon-cayenne vinaigrette.

The standout was the CP bowl: either brown rice or quinoa with light and refreshing veggies, fresh herbs, and an asian flare. We went with the brown rice and added soy-marinated salmon. The sweetness of the marinade was balanced by the tartness of the cucumber, while carrots and peanuts provided a dynamic mix of textures.

Try the popular mint iced tea; it's refreshing on a warm day.

CLEAN BITES
- Must try: CP bowl.

Cuisine:
Vegetarian/Vegan

Neighborhood:
Larchmont, Venice

Meals Served:
Breakfast, Lunch,
Dinner

CAFE GRATITUDE

639 N. Larchmont Blvd.
323-580-6383

cafegratitudela.com
@CafeGratitudeLA

512 Rose Ave.
424-231-8000

cafegratitudevenice.com
@CafeGratitudeVB

Leave your Birkenstocks at home: Cafe Gratitude is vegan, organic food at its most modern and stylish. Hip throngs pack in for flavorful fare and an attitude adjustment.

Just add "I am" before the name of each menu item and you've got yourself a positive affirmation (leave your cynicism with your Birks). Feeling "Fulfilled"? If not, chances are you will be after tucking into this deep bowl of greens and vegetables dressed with fig balsamic. Maybe "Liberated" is more your speed—you'll certainly be freed from the average pasta dish with iodine-rich kelp noodles, heirloom cherry tomatoes and brazil nut parmesan tossed with omega-friendly hemp seed pesto. Take "Fortified" to a new level with one of our go-to favorites: seasonal vegetables over brown rice or quinoa with tangy garlic-tahini sauce.

And the naturally sweetened desserts? Pure "Bliss"—in this case, chocolate cream pie with pecan-date crust.

CLEAN BITES

- Many raw food options available.
- The restaurant's own Be Love Farm supplies most of the produce. Cafe Gratitude also hosts dinners at the farm.
- While many other restaurants say "organic when available," here they say, "if it isn't available then we don't offer it."

CAFÉ PINOT

700 W. 5th St.
213-239-6500

patinagroup.com/
CafePinot
@Patina_Group

Cuisine:
Californian, French

Neighborhood:
Downtown

Meals Served:
Lunch, Dinner

If the skyscrapers of downtown LA weren't surrounding you, you might think you had sauntered into a Parisian scene at Café Pinot. Something about the gorgeous garden patio, set in the plaza right next to the stunning Art Deco public library, feels Old World and très European.

On the plate you can find French classics like French onion soup and flat-iron steak, but more so the offerings reflect the California sensibilities of Joachim Splichal's Patina Group. What's freshest at the local farmers market guides the ever-changing menu.

Count on a bevy of seasonal salads and several seafood selections. If you spot it, definitely opt for the outstanding halibut. There's usually a risotto dish, as well as meat selections ranging from duck to pork chops. The majority of entrées are accompanied by an enticing mixture of expertly cooked veggies. This is special-occasion fare in an evocative setting, perfect for business or romance.

CLEAN BITES

- Must try: Mary's rotisserie chicken, with a dijon mustard glaze, served with crispy fries.
- Dine like a fairy in the outdoor patio during the restaurant's Secret Garden Happy Hour (Monday through Friday, 2:30 p.m. to close, and Saturday, 5 p.m. to close).
- At lunch, the chef offers a two-course market menu of "spa" cuisine, culled from the freshest farmers market ingredients, for $19.95.

Cuisine:
American (Traditional),
Seafood

Neighborhood:
Malibu

Meals Served:
Breakfast, Brunch,
Lunch, Dinner

CARBON BEACH CLUB

22878 Pacific Coast Hwy.
310-456-6444

malibubeachinn.com/
dining
@malibubeachinn

For a taste of the upscale Malibu beach lifestyle, look no further than the open sun deck at the Carbon Beach Club, located at the boutique Malibu Beach Inn. Chef Victor Morales keeps the mix of local and hotel-guest diners happy with dishes that feel right at home as you listen to the waves lapping on the beach below.

There are lots of seafood offerings, and a fried calamari appetizer gets supersized, using thick, 4-inch strips of calamari steak instead of rings. For a non-fried appetizer, the thickly pureed roasted tomato soup is so hearty and satisfying it's like a meal in itself.

Great choices for a relaxed day in the 'Bu include the popular lobster club sandwich, which arrives generously stuffed with large lobster chunks, wild arugula and garlic. The vegetarian burger's flavorful vegan patty is made with roasted corn and beans, then cooked until crisp around the edges and given extra heft with chunky guacamole. The menu keeps things light and breezy, with several green salads sourced from local farms and tangy ceviche made daily with the seasonal fish of the day.

CLEAN BITES

- If you've only got time to grab a power breakfast before hitting the waves, stop in for freshly squeezed juices and smoothies made from organic and naturally sweetened ingredients served right on the beach.
- The wine list focuses on limited-edition, small-production bottles from California wineries.
- Gluten-free, vegan and vegetarian dishes are noted on the menu.

CHAYA

Multiple locations

thechaya.com
@chayarestaurant

Cuisine:
French, Japanese

Meals Served:
Lunch, Dinner

Can't decide whether to go out for French food or Japanese? At Chaya, you don't have to. This arty brasserie has a split personality that shuttles between Europe and Asia. The elegant, high-ceiling dining room draws on the strong sense of aesthetics in both French and Japanese culture, with accents such as towering bamboo stalks and Impressionist paintings.

Dishes are as beautifully composed as they are thoughtfully executed—and many are drive-across-town delicious. Our spicy tuna rolls were given a tart, colorful twist with a topping of jade-hued wasabi tobiko. We would return again and again for the buttery miso sea bass, a juicy filet swimming in beurre blanc and topped with hijiki rice and broccolini.

European-inspired plates range from classic French onion soup to seasonal salads to steak and chicken dishes. Whether you lean toward Paris or Tokyo, the common denominator amid all the fusion is the locally sourced produce.

CLEAN BITES

- A chalkboard mounted in the dining room displays farms the restaurant is currently sourcing from.

Cuisine:
Italian

Neighborhood:
West Hollywood

Meals Served:
Breakfast, Lunch,
Dinner

CHEEBO

7533 W. Sunset Blvd.   cheebo.com
323-850-7070   @Cheebolicious

With multicolored stained-glass windows and bright orange walls covered with eclectic art, Cheebo is no shrinking violet. Its bold décor is matched by a perky scene and feel-good Cal-Italian fare. Despite the audacious vibe, the restaurant is humble in its concern for the planet; it takes sustainable sourcing seriously.

Many diners head straight for the artisanal pizzas, uniquely oblong in shape and served on wood planks. On our visit we loved the sumptuous sausage and fennel pie—tender chunks of fennel help us feel less guilty about all that sausage-y goodness. Homemade lasagna also scratches the hearty Italian itch.

But it's possible to sidestep heavy carbs. Fresh vegetable salads, the grilled artichoke starter and entrées like cedar plank-roasted salmon prove light and clean. Wild-card selections like brisket sandwiches and lamb tagine with harissa bust out of the typical Italian mold, which Cheebo does on every level.

CLEAN BITES

- Try combining a few sides, like the salmon, quinoa and seasonal market veggies for a super-healthful meal.
- All packaging is recyclable or biodegradable.

CHEZ MÉLANGE

1611 S. Catalina Ave.
310-540-1222

chezmelange.com
@ChezMelange

Cuisine:
Californian

Neighborhood:
Redondo Beach

Meals Served:
Brunch, Dinner

Wander to the back of the gastropub Bouzy and you'll find Chez Mélange, an elegant room with fine art, low lighting and high-concept fare. The market-driven menu highlights world cuisines, while a seafood cart rolls through the dining room showcasing fresh catches. It's the epitome of "think global, eat local."

The offerings rotate frequently, reflecting the kitchen's commitment to seasonal sourcing. Outstanding pan-seared New England scallops might be dressed with cauliflower puree and blood orange gastrique one week, then bacon mashed potatoes and maple butter the next. Pork belly can get the Cajun treatment with pecans and wild mushroom grits (Cajun cooking is chef Robert Bell's specialty), or a fruity backyard BBQ makeover with plum sauce, melon and currant slaw.

Fresh veggies make up the largest section on the menu, from Asian-style shishito peppers to Italianate fava beans with ricotta salata. This kind of variety makes the gastronomy a true mélange.

CLEAN BITES

- The restaurant sources some of its produce from the Seed to Plate program at Palos Verdes High School, where special-education students maintain a garden.
- The owners produce their own wine, a chardonnay and a pinot noir crafted to complement their food, in partnership with a local winery.
- For a less formal experience, head to the front room and patio and experience Bouzy, Chez Mélange's on-site gastropub.

Cuisine:
Mexican

Meals Served:
Lunch, Dinner

CHIPOTLE

Multiple locations

chipotle.com
@ChipotleTweets

With the tagline "Farm-to-Face," Chipotle takes the farm-to-table concept, wraps it in a tortilla and gets it to your mouth with impressive speed and flavor.

The customizable burritos and tacos are built from quality ingredients that reflect the chain's dedication to "food with integrity"—that is, produce and proteins raised with respect for the animals, the environment and the farmers.

Join the assembly-line queue and be ready to declare your choice of protein (no dawdling!): either braised carnitas or barbacoa, or adobo-marinated and grilled chicken or steak. (Vegetarians can select grilled red onions and green bell peppers.) Top it with cilantro-lime rice and pinto or black beans, and calibrate the addition of super-fresh guacamole, cheese, sour cream and/or salsa to your liking.

As the burritos are humongous, try building your own salad or burrito bowl instead.

CLEAN BITES

- Chipotle recently switched its cooking oil from soybean to sunflower to reduce reliance on genetically modified foods.
- The majority of dairy products used come from pasture-raised cows.
- The chain created its own Food With Integrity program to work with smaller, family owned farms and to ensure the quality of their produce, animal products and beans.

CHURCH & STATE

1850 Industrial St., #100
213-405-1434

churchandstatebistro.com
@ChurchStateLA

Cuisine:
French

Neighborhood:
Downtown

Meals Served:
Lunch, Dinner

This convivial urban bistro is like something lifted straight from Paris—except it doesn't rely on heavy cream and butter to execute exquisite dishes.

Design accents like smoky mirrors and chalkboards are squarely Parisian, while industrial features like brick floors and exposed ducts give away the space's former use as a National Biscuit Co. loading dock. But lively tables, oodles of French wine bottles (many organic and biodynamic) and strings of Edison bulbs glowing overhead impart an ebullient vibe.

You might start off with the escargot appetizer, redolent of garlic, move onto one of the seasonal vegetable salads, and finish with the light yet satisfying bouillabaisse, loaded with prawns, manila clams, mussels, fennel, potatoes and leeks.

On the heartier end, the beef is grass-fed, which makes the steak frites less guilt-provoking. A rarity for a French restaurant, vegetarians have several choices including a veggie plate and vegetable sides.

CLEAN BITES

- Must try: The trout meuniere is a standout dish and can be prepared gluten-free upon request.
- The menu has a large variety of organic and biodynamic wines.

COOKS COUNTY

8009 Beverly Blvd.
323-653-8009

cookscounty
restaurant.com
@CooksCounty

If it wasn't for the glowing Edison bulbs, urbane red accent wall and jazzy soundtrack, you might think this rustic restaurant was located in the countryside. The eats couldn't be more farm fresh, and decorative touches like sheaves of dried wheat and the servers' burlap aprons call to mind a farmhouse kitchen.

Changing daily, the menu is an opus of produce-driven American fare. We relished the starter of heirloom radishes with lemon butter and crunchy salt—a brilliant alternative to bread and butter. Picked-at-peak peaches paired lusciously with blue cheese, toasted pecans, chopped endive and frilly watercress.

Our tender, grass-fed beef was braised for five hours. Our favorite dish was Idaho trout dressed lightly with brown butter, crunchy almonds and a dusting of herbs. It had the kind of pure, smoky taste of campfire cooking. Even simple vegetable sides like roasted fingerling potatoes and sprouting broccoli were flat-out exceptional.

CLEAN BITES

- Farm-to-Taco Tuesdays put a Mexican spin on healthy comfort fare.
- Cooks County takes sustainable sourcing seriously—just check out the list of local farms and ranchers it supports, printed on the daily menu.
- Olive oil is used exclusively for cooking, and cold-pressed nut oils are used for finishing.

CORAL TREE CAFÉ

Multiple locations   coraltreecafe.com
@CoralTreeCafe

Cuisine:
American (Casual)

Meals Served:
Breakfast, Lunch,
Dinner

With an order-at-the-counter format, Coral Tree is quite casual, but there's nothing blasé about its commitment to "honest food"—organic ingredients and healthy preparations. The farmhouse-inspired restaurant induces mania at weekend brunch hour, when fanatics descend for the organic egg dishes and stuffed French toast.

At lunch and dinner, when crowds are thinner, the menu is a bit heavy on white flour, with sandwiches and pastas dominating the menu. If you indulge, skip the turkey bolognese pasta and go for the steak panini—grilled hanger steak, barbecued onions, avocado and provolone—or the rosemary chicken sandwich with brie and pear.

Salads, like the gargantuan orchard salad with Granny Smith apples, grapes, cucumbers and caramelized walnuts, showcase the über-fresh produce. We also dig the vegan veggie wrap—a nutty whole-wheat wrap stuffed with cabbage, sprouts, avocado and tomatoes, with house-made hummus. Cap it off with fresh juice or organic coffee.

CLEAN BITES

- Need to work as you chow down? Take advantage of the free Wi-Fi.
- Coral Tree is a Certified Green Restaurant by the Green Restaurant Association.

Cuisine:
American
(Contemporary)

Neighborhood:
Century City

Meals Served:
Lunch, Dinner

CRAFT

10100 Constellation Blvd.   craftrestaurantsinc.com
310-279-4180   @CraftLA

Despite the celeb-chef factor (at the helm is Top Chef judge Tom Colicchio) and the heavy-hitting clientele (CAA agents from the building next door come for power lunches), there are few theatrics on the plate at this NYC transplant. The kitchen embraces elegant understatement in its approach to seasonal, contemporary American cooking.

Floating filament bulbs are the single flourish in the wood-and-earth-toned dining room, and the menu—whose items are often described in no more than one or two words—is minimalist. You definitely need to consult your knowledgeable server to find out more about preparations, which change frequently.

Quail, which on our visit was burnished with sherry and wild blueberry reduction and partnered with roasted figs, is a standout among the meat and fish options. Vegetables are handled with utmost care, whether roasted, sautéed or tossed into mixed salads. We're christening this craft the "SS Simply Delicious".

CLEAN BITES

- Must try: The avocado, tomatillo and spiced peanut salad is a stunning combination.
- The menu lists the farmers Craft partners with.
- Check out Tom Colicchio's TEDx talk on hunger, food policy and voting on food issues.

CROSSROADS KITCHEN

8284 Melrose Ave.　　crossroadskitchen.com
323-782-9245　　@Crossroads8284

Cuisine:
Mediterranean, Small
Plates, Vegetarian/
Vegan

Neighborhood:
Beverly Grove

Meals Served:
Brunch, Lunch, Dinner

At Tal Ronnen's Crossroads, plant-based ingredients truly shine. This is not your usual casual vegan spot—the attention to presentation is a reminder to forgo the Havaianas and make a reservation in advance.

And boy is it worth it. The lentil flatbread is fantastic: A warm, soft stack arrives with three seasonal spreads. The artichoke oysters wasn't our favorite, but the watermelon salad was a refreshing treat—the almond cheese and pistachios provide savory texture against the sweet melon and tomatoes.

It's hard to pick a single standout dish, as the crab cakes and wood-fired meaty lasagna were equally delicious—so close to the "real" thing that both vegans and meat-lovers will revel in them.

CLEAN BITES

- Ronnen is author of the *New York Times* best-seller *The Conscious Cook* and prepared the meals for Oprah's 21-day cleanse. He has also cooked for Bill Clinton.
- In addition to the elegant central dining room, the restaurant features an artisanal cheese shop, a wine room with a retractable roof, and an original Toulouse-Lautrec print.
- You can now order lunch online if you don't have time to dine (pick up only).

Cuisine:
Italian

Neighborhood:
Beverly Hills

Meals Served:
Breakfast, Brunch,
Lunch, Dinner

CULINA

300 S. Doheny Drive
310-860-4000

culinarestaurant.com
@CulinaLA

Although it's ensconced in the Four Seasons Hotel Los Angeles, Culina is a refreshing departure from the stuffy hotel restaurant scene. Gone are the sky-high floral arrangements and hovering maitre'd in favor of an elegant bar, warmly lit dining room and lush outdoor patio.

The Italian fare, too, twists expectations. Traditional dishes are given a light makeover, with an emphasis on produce-driven preparations. Sure, there are pizzas and pastas, but it's easy to skip these carb-heavy dishes when the frequently rotating veggies and proteins are so ethereal. We'd start with the cappesante, thinly sliced raw diver scallops with a subtle citrusy sauce, and move on to one of the bright salads like barbabietole (chopped roasted beets).

As for main dishes, there are ample meat and seafood selections, the branzino with tomatoes, capers and lemon being a standout. Load up on perfectly cooked, seasonal veggie sides to your heart's content.

CLEAN BITES

- Belly up to the crudo bar for raw selections and cocktails.
- Design your own fresh juice from locally sourced sustainable ingredients.
- Vegan and gluten-free selections are marked on the menu.

THE CURIOUS PALATE

12034 Venice Blvd.
310-437-0144

thecuriouspalate.com
@curious_palate

395 Santa Monica Place
310-395-2901

Cuisine:
Californian

Neighborhood:
Mar Vista, Santa
Monica

Meals Served:
Breakfast, Lunch,
Dinner

This sunny gourmet market-cum-cafe is a foodie paradise. It's the kind of place you can dash into for house-made pickles and olive oils and pastas and legumes from around the world, and then stay for an artisanal, local farm-to-table meal.

Typically such market-cafes tend toward European flavors, and while you can certainly find French and Italian selections on the menu here, the cuisine is more eclectic, jumping from Thai satay salads and Vietnamese báhn mi to shrimp po'boys and Casablanca grilled steak and harissa sandwiches.

Salads are perhaps our favorite dishes here, and the lineup changes seasonally. The Big Curious salad features a beautiful medley of baby greens, olives and marinated beets, plus deliciously tender, not-your-mother's lima beans. We're also a fan of the tofu-free lentil-chickpea veggie burger.

Inventive tacos, hearty pastas and comfort-food plates supremely satisfy at the dinner hour, while breakfast scrambles and griddle items get the day started deliciously.

CLEAN BITES

- Must try: the salads. They are all made from produce fresh from local markets.
- Take home some artisanal treats. The Curious Palate is also a marketplace.

Cuisine:
American (Casual)

Neighborhood:
Redondo Beach

Meals Served:
Breakfast, Lunch,
Dinner

DOMA KITCHEN

420 N. Pacific Coast Hwy.
310-372-7298
310-372-7240

domakitchencafe.com
@DomaKitchen

Wandering and hungry in Redondo Beach? Search no further. Take a pause at Doma Kitchen, where you can sit in an outdoor patio and take in some local art and a satisfying meal.

Doma means "home" in Slavic, and hints of the owners' Eastern European background as well as their global travel is peppered throughout the menu. Breakfast is served all day (they use cage-free eggs), so we started with the popular pancetta scramble, which included a good balance of Italian bacon and scallions. The veggie omelet sandwich is exactly what it sounds like, but we were pleased to find we truly got our veggie fill, as the eggs were stuffed with bell peppers, zucchini and tomatoes. The salads feature locally sourced produce, and even the bread is organic, thanks to daily deliveries from Bread Los Angeles.

Doma Kitchen certainly provides a homey atmosphere al fresco, and, as such, the service can be a bit relaxed. Expect a wait before getting to bask in their "glocal" cuisine.

CLEAN BITES

- The restaurant has dog-friendly amenities!
- The kitchen uses filtered water for cooking and alkaline water is provided for all beverages.
- The patio itself is a piece of art. All furniture has been repurposed, including the recycled denim pillow covers. The communal wood tables are built from salvaged beams, and the vintage metal chairs and tables have been given a new life.

ELF CAFE

2135 Sunset Blvd.
213-484-6829

elfcafe.com
@elfcafe

Cuisine:
Mediterranean,
Vegetarian/Vegan

Neighborhood:
Echo Park

Meals Served:
Dinner

This handsome, intimate Echo Park cafe turns vegetarian dining into a special occasion. What began as a 700-square-foot space that relied on hot plates to get the cooking done has evolved into a "real" kitchen that has expanded into a neighboring storefront. But Elf has preserved the DIY ethos, which accounts for the droves of hipsters vying for a seat.

It doesn't hurt that the menu is mostly vegan and gluten-free, and that chef/owner Scott Zwiezen is a stickler for sustainability. Or that exposed brick walls and candlelight scream romance. But none of that would matter, we suppose, if the food wasn't delicious. And it is.

The seasonally fluctuating salads, small plates and mains are inspired by the Eastern Mediterranean. You might start with baked sheep feta wrapped in vine leaves, munch on a spicy Moroccan kale salad with house harissa and move on to a market vegetable tagine over quinoa. Opa!

CLEAN BITES

- The cheeses are free of animal rennet and sourced from small, local producers.
- All of the water is reverse-osmosis-treated.

Cuisine:
Raw, Vegetarian/Vegan

Neighborhood:
Santa Monica

Meals Served:
Breakfast, Lunch,
Dinner

EUPHORIA LOVES RAWVOLUTION

2301 Main St.
310-392-9501

euphorialoves
rawvolution.com
@rawvolution

If the "rawvolution" were televised, it would definitely happen at Euphoria Loves Rawvolution, a camera-ready cafe where the raw and the beautiful commingle. Westside yogis and health-nut celebs flock here for creative plant-based dishes and natural juice fixes a stone's throw from the beach.

The approach to raw food preparation here is innovative, with culinary sleights-of-hand like the Chips and Bacon burger. The savory nut/seed burger on tender onion bread boasts coconut "jerky" instead of actual bacon, with a side of zesty kale chips. Other dishes are more straightforward, like the Holy Macro bowl (a bevy of kale studded with "nofu" and drizzled with red pepper tahini) and the Superfood soup (a spicy, slurp-worthy stew of cucumber, nori and avocado).

Rolls, pizzas and Mexican specialties round out the menu. Wash it all down with a cold-pressed juice or smoothie. If you're short on time, grab your beverage at the sidewalk window.

CLEAN BITES

- The restaurant is a community center for those living a raw food lifestyle, with a retail store, workshops, cookbooks and delivery service.
- Food scraps are composted for reuse as fertilizer and fuel.
- To-go packaging is biodegradable, and only non-toxic cleaning supplies are used.

EVO KITCHEN

7950 W. Sunset Blvd., #104   evokitchenla.com
323-375-3390   @EVOkitchenla

Cuisine:
Italian

Neighborhood:
West Hollywood

Meals Served:
Lunch, Dinner

Not your average pizza joint, EVO Kitchen caters to diners of all dietary needs, hopes and desires. The gluten-avoidant can relish their tasty gluten-free pizza crusts, which are nearly indistinguishable from the traditional pies, and vegans can gobble up the delicious "V for Vegan" veggie pie while sidestepping meat and dairy (skip the soy cheese, though).

Special dieters can bring along their "meat lovin' gluten grubbin" friends, too, as pizza choices include everything from antibiotic- and hormone-free classic pepperoni to seasoned ground beef.

Fresh produce is also abundant. Healthy starters like a collection of raw veggies with light hummus and zesty-sweet fig and olive tapenade are on offer, and try one of our favorite pies, the pear-and-gorgonzola finished with olive oil.

Veggie-driven wraps and salads round out the much-more-than-pizza menu, while local craft beers (some gluten-free!) and sustainable wines keep things festive.

CLEAN BITES

- The eco-friendly restaurant is built to LEED specs.
- The kitchen only cooks with olive oil.

Cuisine:
Middle Eastern,
Vegetarian/Vegan

Neighborhood:
Fairfax

Meals Served:
Lunch, Dinner

FALA BAR

7751 1/2 Melrose Ave.
323-424-7131

falabar.com
@falabar

Three cheers for the chickpea! This organic, vegan, grab-and-go spot specializes in made-to-order falafel (in original, sweet potato, spicy and crunchy varieties) stuffed into sandwiches or scattered on salads made with produce from local farms.

The tiny storefront can only accommodate a couple of people ordering at the counter, so grab a sidewalk table or munch your sandwich while window shopping on funky Melrose.

This is a paradise for the gluten-averse, who can enjoy everything on the menu except the pita bread. The tabouli is made with quinoa, and the cabbage-leaf wrap option is a novel alternative to the traditional pita pocket—and a great way to get your greens! We swooned over the crispy-outside, soft-inside sweet potato falafel as well as the "Fala Me To KALEifornia" salad, loaded with locally sourced lemony kale, purple cabbage and avocado topped with creamy house-made hummus. Skip the spicy carrots and go for the smoky baba ghanoush.

CLEAN BITES

- The falafel is baked, not fried.
- The menu features all-alkaline, organic produce.
- Fala uses biodegradable containers and cutlery for salads and to-go items.

THE FARMER'S KITCHEN

1555 Vine St., Suite 119
323-467-7600

www.seela.org/
farmerskitchen
@HollywoodFK

Cuisine:
American (Casual)

Neighborhood:
Hollywood

Meals Served:
Breakfast, Brunch,
Lunch

If you can't wait to get home from the weekly Sunday Hollywood Farmers Market before stealing a taste of all-natural goodness, then pop into The Farmer's Kitchen, an adjacent brick-and-mortar establishment that prepares market-fresh meals from local vendors every Sunday.

Jars of locally produced jam, honey and tomato sauce can be enjoyed in-house or at home. Buttered toast with artisanal preserves is on offer at breakfast, and on our visit the house-made marinara sauce was employed to delicious effect in a tender organic chicken parmigiana sandwich.

Aside from preserved produce, there are abundant fresh options that drive the seasonally fluctuating menus. At breakfast, the side of greens with your egg dish might be sautéed Swiss chard and spinach with addictive ginger-garlic sauce. Fresh salad choices at lunch might include a colorful cherry tomato salad with crumbled feta. The heirloom cherry tomato on top? Proceeds benefit local farmers.

CLEAN BITES

- The facility is also used for educational and training purposes that support community awareness about healthy eating.
- The Farmer's Kitchen gets its ingredients from the farmers market outside its door—bringing farm-to-table dining to a whole new level.
- A pop-up restaurant, Field Trip, will be occupying the space in 2015.

Cuisine:
Californian

Neighborhood:
Santa Monica

Meals Served:
Breakfast, Brunch,
Lunch, Dinner

FARMSHOP

225 26th St., Suite 25
310-566-2400

farmshopca.com
@FarmshopLA

True to its name, Farmshop displays an exemplary dedication to sustainable farm-to-table dining.

Many of the menu items are named after the farms from which the food has come. The Milliken Family Farm cucumber salad, composed of insanely fresh cucumbers, smoked Idaho trout, blueberries, and a tart, creamy yogurt dill dressing, was dazzling. The Stracciatella cheese appetizer featured a generous serving of this tangy, runny cheese, accompanied by stone fruit jam, pink peppercorns and whole-wheat toasts. The wild striped bass was flaky and perfectly cooked atop a summer squash caponata, olives, pine nuts and basil. All the dishes were standouts, but the prime beef eye of ribeye was killer. Expertly seared beef was dressed up with figs, spaetzle, porcini mushrooms and shishito peppers.

No time to dine? You can still experience the brilliance of Farmshop by visiting its adjacent market, where you can grab some lunch to-go as well as an array of artisanal, local goods.

CLEAN BITES

- Must try: Farmshop's fries have been called "the best in LA." The potatoes are from Weiser Farm and fried in rice bran oil instead of your typical GMO fat.
- Browse Farmshop's website to see a complete list of the sustainable purveyors it works with.
- Farmshop is so committed to its sourcing practices that it has its own specialty buyer, forager and educator on staff.

FIG

101 Wilshire Blvd.
310-319-3111

figsantamonica.com
@FigSantaMonica

Cuisine:
Californian

Neighborhood:
Santa Monica

Meals Served:
Breakfast, Brunch,
Lunch, Dinner

Taking its name from the voluptuous fruit, Fig turns nature's bounty into a delightfully sensual culinary experience. The casually elegant restaurant is tucked away on the ground floor of the Fairmont Miramar Hotel, but its set-up—with a pewter bar and charcuterie station—is inviting for locals and out-of-towners alike.

Fresh, seasonal produce guides the menu, so it's perpetually rotating. Small plates abound, perfect for sharing. Our "blistered" little gem romaine hearts salad was pleasingly savory—singed on all edges, salted with white anchovies and nutty Reggiano cheese. We also enjoyed the tanginess of the marinated young beet salad and the fluffiness of the scarlet quinoa studded with marcona almonds.

Proteins can be hit or miss; on our visit, golden raisins and tangerines overpowered our scallops' delicate, natural sweetness. But our lamb medallions with slow-roasted tomatoes were mouthwatering. When the kitchen sticks to unfussy preparations, it's pure bliss.

CLEAN BITES

- Adventurous palates will enjoy the restaurant's Feed Me! program. Chef Ray Garcia will prepare a custom combination of current Fig favorites and off-menu surprises for the table.
- The chef personally scours the Santa Monica Farmers Market each week for produce.
- The restaurant has a dedicated forager, who is charged with visiting farms throughout the state to procure the tastiest organically grown fruits, veggies and specialty foods.

Cuisine:
Californian

Neighborhood:
Venice

Meals Served:
Breakfast, Lunch,
Dinner

FIGTREE'S CAFÉ & GRILL

429 Ocean Front Walk   figtreescafe.com

310-392-4937

With its health-oriented menu and front-row ticket to the wacky Venice Beach boardwalk action, Figtree's retains a funky 1970s vibe that has made it a local institution since 1978.

The cottage-like interior space is comfortable, but a spot on the wraparound patio is where you want to be. The views of surf and sand might inspire a craving for seafood, and you can't go wrong with the chunky crab cakes with mango salsa, ahi tuna on inventive rosemary skewers, or Adolpho's tacos filled with seasonal fish and exceptional guacamole.

Comfort-food favorites like sandwiches, burgers and stir-fries get a healthy twist. We found the tofu Reuben to be a delightfully light version of the classic sandwich. Breakfast is also a celebrated event here—so much so that it's served all day. But the tasty eggs benedict is available only on weekends and holidays, so plan to brave the crowds for a taste.

CLEAN BITES

- Must try: Figtree's signature Navajo corncakes—slightly sweet corncakes topped with black bean chili, salsa, feta and avocado.
- Get 50% off breakfast from 8 to 9 a.m. every day except holidays.

FLORE VEGAN

3818 W. Sunset Blvd.
323-953-0611

florevegan.com
@FloreVegan

Cuisine:
Vegetarian/Vegan

Neighborhood:
Silver Lake

Meals Served:
Breakfast, Brunch,
Lunch, Dinner

For those who love animal-free food and hip people-watching, this trendy, all-vegan spot is the place to be. A small sidewalk cafe, Flore boasts cute, vintage-inspired interiors and a charming outdoor seating area.

Don't let its petite size fool you, though; the menu is large and varied. Weekend brunchers pack in for the dense, tasty, blueberry buckwheat pancakes with crunchy walnut bits and sweet, gooey blueberry sauce. Pair them with the smoky tempeh bacon, a cut above the typical faux breakfast meat both from a taste and nutritional standpoint.

Lunch and dinner options range from burritos to sandwiches. The salads are big, fresh and creative; the grapefruit, avocado and fennel salad has the kind of tangy, citrusy flavor that will leave you feeling refreshed and energized. Burgers are on the ho-hum side, but we relished the juicy portobello mushroom tacos on corn tortillas.

Save room for naturally sweetened and wheat-free desserts like the decadent apple cinnamon cake.

CLEAN BITES

- The cafe doubles as a fresh juice, smoothie and tea tonic bar as well as a deli counter.
- The kitchen uses organic tofu and tempeh.
- The menu features interesting and unique vegan options, so we recommend going with a few people and sharing a variety of dishes.

Cuisine:
American (Casual)

Neighborhood:
West LA

Meals Served:
Breakfast, Lunch

FOOD

10571 Pico Blvd.   food-la.com
310-441-7770

As its name suggests, Food is all about the basics. The bustling, order-at-the-counter market and cafe, housed in a bright, tomato-red cube of a space, focuses on simple yet high-quality fundamentals including soups, salads, sandwiches and breakfast fare.

But basic doesn't mean boring. Case in point: The slow-roasted beef tenderloin sandwich comes on a crunchy French baguette smeared with garlic-onion jam—the perfect backdrop for spicy arugula leaves and a dollop of horseradish cream. Definitely not your average steak sandwich!

The cafe's reliance on seasonal, organic ingredients means that menu offerings change regularly. You'll find a burger of the day—topped with caramelized onions and paired with paprika-spiced potato wedges—and two daily soups. Both our Tuscan white bean and vegan roasted heirloom tomato soups were superb.

Sweet and savory breakfasts are so popular they're offered all day long. In a rush? Take some delectable deli salads to-go.

CLEAN BITES

- Must try: the "deconstructed" Cobb salad, a dazzling display of cubed, herbed chicken breast, egg, crispy bacon, tomato, avocado and a lighter-than-most blue cheese dressing.
- The cafe doubles as a market where you can pick up wine, cheese and prepared foods.
- They use organic tofu.

FOODLAB

3206 W. Sunset Blvd.
323-661-2666

foodlab-la.com
@FoodLab

7253 Santa Monica Blvd.
323-851-7120

Dining at FoodLab is a bit like going on a haute picnic: The thick wood tables and gourmet sandwiches, salads and sides bring to mind a sophisticated, alfresco "nosh sesh." Upping the haute factor is the famous clientele, such as Gwen Stefani and Naomi Campbell. Co-owner Esther Linsmayer is a former Parisian model, not to mention Le Cordon Bleu graduate.

That pedigree might explain why the food is not only good looking but also great tasting. The sandwiches tempt with inventive layers of fresh ingredients. We delighted in the grilled organic chicken BLT accented by creamy aioli and arugula on crusty ciabatta. Even better was the wholesome garden sandwich, a five-grain masterpiece with seemingly just-plucked cucumbers, watercress, carrots and tomato.

Also try the well-stocked cheese plate with dried fruits and nuts—perfectly composed for a picnic in the park.

CLEAN BITES

- Going on an actual picnic? Let FoodLab pack a box for you. Each box includes a sandwich of your choice, a vegan salad and a daily side.
- The environmentally friendly plates, cutlery, cups and packaging are biodegradable.

Cuisine:
Californian

Neighborhood:
Silver Lake

Meals Served:
Lunch, Dinner

FORAGE

3823 W. Sunset Blvd.
323-663-6885

foragela.com
@Foragela

Backyard gardeners: at attention! This gourmet deli smack in the middle of Silver Lake supplements its farmers market-procured produce with the spoils of approved LA home growers' fruit trees and vegetable gardens. Now that's what we call locally sourced!

The kitchen works wonders with all those seasonal goodies, putting out a daily changing array of beautiful deli salads displayed at the counter. We relished our kale-arugula salad with a cool lemon-garlic vinaigrette, as well as a hearty barley salad with sweet-and-sour agro dolce sauce.

You can make a meal from the salads or pair yours with a healthy protein like grilled salmon or Petaluma organic, free-range chicken cooked in the rotisserie. Robust sandwiches, quiches, bowls and daily specials complete the casual, quick-service menu. Seating is limited, and the place gets crowded at the lunch hour, so plan accordingly or take your order to-go (and enjoy in your own backyard).

CLEAN BITES

- Interested in urban farming? Go to the restaurant's website to read about the home growers who help supply Forage.
- Chef/owner Jason Kim previously cooked at Lucques (p. 125).
- Bring farm-fresh dishes to your next event—Forage caters.

FOUR CAFE

2122 Colorado Blvd.
323-550-1988

fourcafe.net
@FourCafe

519 S. Fairfax
323-272-3993

Husband-wife duo Michelle and Corey Wilton put a fresh, healthy spin on the casual neighborhood cafe at this something-for-everyone spot. Head chef Michelle previously cooked at such rarified LA restaurants as L'Orangerie, Patina and Sona, and her penchant for top-notch ingredients and gourmet presentation is evident even in the down-to-earth fare here.

The seasonal menu of soups, salads, sandwiches and small plates has a flexitarian mentality, with a chimichurri steak sandwich listed alongside a tempeh BLTA. We're wild for the Hawaiian BBQ pork sandwich, loaded with sweet mango barbecue sauce and napa cabbage in a house-made bun.

Organic free-range chicken, grass-fed steak or wild salmon can be added to any of the salads, where the combination of greens, veggies, nuts and cheeses run the gamut from Mediterranean to Southwestern to Asian flavors. Breakfast brings egg dishes, tofu scrambles and lemon ricotta pancakes.

CLEAN BITES

- The restaurant is committed to buying locally from farmers markets, and the kitchen takes a slow food approach to cooking.
- Organic tempeh and tofu are served.
- Four Cafe's green business practices include the use of reclaimed wood in the dining room, used equipment in the kitchen and energy efficient appliances.

GOLDIE'S

8422 W. 3rd St.
323-677-2470

goldiesla.com
@GoldiesLA

Goldie's is a den of culinary comforts, circa 1972. But while the wood paneling and Mexican rugs provide a vintage vibe, the food is modern.

The diver scallops were delicious, prepared with brown butter and sea grass—we wish the portion size was a bit larger. The ricotta and honey-drenched grilled flatbread was out of this world. The wild salmon was cooked with enough heat to keep the exterior crispy and the flesh moist. Served with a dollop of cauliflower puree and shaved cucumber, it was satisfying.

The standout dish was the hanger steak. It provided a generous serving of expertly seared beef atop a bed of enoki mushrooms and leeks that gave the meat a smoky burst of umami.

All dishes confirmed that the kitchen has mastered the art of grilling proteins and puts a forward spin on classic food.

CLEAN BITES

- The food comes from farms that employ biodynamic or sustainable farming methods, and Goldie's also supports winemakers who produce small batches by the same methods.
- Goldie's serves filtered water, recycles, and relies on Ecolab for all of its cleaning products.

GRACIAS MADRE

8905 Melrose Ave.
323-978-2170

graciasmadreweho.com
@GMWeHo

Cuisine:
Mexican, Vegetarian/
Vegan

Neighborhood:
West Hollywood

Meals Served:
Brunch, Lunch, Dinner

Dining at this haute yet homey vegan Mexican spot is a little like having a meal at your most stylish friend's hacienda. Tasteful tilework and textiles add south-of-the-border pizzazz to the bustling indoor space, while the sprawling patio boasts a wood-burning fireplace and fairy lights amid mature olive trees.

From the same team that owns Cafe Gratitude (p. 80), this San Francisco transplant gives Mexican classics from enchiladas to flautas a 100% organic, veggie-driven makeover.

House-made corn tortillas are a satisfying canvas for an array of dishes. In a trio of tacos, seared cauliflower topped with cashew crema was our favorite filling. From dish to dish, the flavor profiles can be a bit monotone; zesty alternatives include tamales stuffed with poblano peppers, and "chorizo" mushrooms paired with butternut squash and cilantro pesto.

Can't snag a reservation? Join the hip throng vying for agave-based cocktails and eat at the bar.

CLEAN BITES

- Must try: the mild, chunky guacamole, simply seasoned with onion and lime.
- The restaurant's organic produce comes primarily from co-founder Terces Engelhart's Be Love Farm in Vacaville.
- Gracias Madre launched the Seed Initiative project to preserve non-GMO heritage corn varieties.

Cuisine:
American (Casual)

Neighborhood:
Burbank, Glendale

Meals Served:
Breakfast, Lunch,
Dinner

GRANVILLE CAFÉ

121 N. San Fernando Blvd.   granvillecafe.com
818-848-4726   @GranvilleCafe

807 Americana Way
818-550-0472

If you're shopping downtown Burbank or The Americana at Brand, this eager-to-please neighborhood cafe offers a more healthful and more upscale dining experience than the mall food court ever could. Earth tones, chocolate brown accents and lots of natural wood create a stylish setting that complements the earthy menu.

The something-for-everyone lineup is grounded in the soup-salad-sandwich trifecta. We lapped up the exceptional butternut squash soup, a puddle of liquid gold garnished with dried cranberries and chopped walnuts. The chipotle chicken club, with its spicy aioli, also proved drool-worthy.

Big plates offer heartier options for a more complete meal. One of our go-to favorites is the pan-seared rainbow trout with a light crust of crushed pumpkin seeds, doused in puckery preserved-lemon and butter sauce and served with herbed grilled vegetables. It's the kind of place that works equally well for a quick lunch break or a more relaxed end-of-day wind-down.

CLEAN BITES

- Must try: lettuce cups filled with a vibrant mixture of crimson cherry tomatoes, fresh avocado slices, deep red cabbage and fresh mango.
- The music is curated to span generations, bringing people together over the tunes as well as the food.

GREENLEAF GOURMET CHOPSHOP

9671 Wilshire Blvd.
310-246-0765

greenleafchopshop.com
@greenleaftweets

1888 Century Park E.
424-239-8700

Cuisine:
Californian

Neighborhood:
Beverly Hills,
Century City

Meals Served:
Breakfast, Lunch,
Dinner

Greenleaf is another fresh, delicious addition to the quick-service, salad-driven dining landscape. With its exhibition kitchen and wood-and-chrome decor accents, it's a stylish one, too.

The generously sized salad creations with Scarborough Farms greens live up to the cafe's middle name, with tasty updates on classics. Zorra the Great twists the traditional Greek salad with the addition of spicy arugula and marinated artichokes. The Mexplosion is a novel, flavorful blend of grilled sweet corn, black beans, cilantro, avocado and sunflower seeds.

If you don't see a combo that appeals, the build-your-own option can accommodate any taste and dietary preference. Flame-grilled proteins can be added to any salad, and the sandwich and pizza options will satisfy carb cravings. Don't miss the vegetable sides, either. Selections change seasonally, but we enjoyed the hearty, autumnal roasted beets, yams and walnuts with goat cheese.

CLEAN BITES

- Must try: A bit decadent, we know, but the turkey melt on pretzel bread with aged cheddar, spinach, caramelized onion and truffle oil is worth it.
- The cafe doubles as a fresh fruit-and-veggie juice bar.
- Frequent visitor? Ask about their customer loyalty program to continue eating clean on the cheap.

Cuisine:
American
(Contemporary),
French

Neighborhood:
Hollywood

Meals Served:
Dinner

HATFIELD'S

6703 Melrose Ave.
323-935-2977

hatfieldsrestaurant.com

This sleek, ambitious restaurant from husband-wife team Karen and Quinn Hatfield sets the bar for seasonal Cal-French fare in Los Angeles. Hatfield's is destination dining, replete with white tablecloths, elaborate tasting menus and sophisticated wine pairings.

The multi-course prix-fixe offerings, which change with the seasons and are available in both vegetarian and carnivorous iterations, will please adventurous diners who want to sample the best of what's currently cooking. But the a la carte selections make it possible to design your own meal, too.

We found the signature croque madame—yellowtail sashimi and prosciutto sandwiched between two pieces of grilled brioche, topped with a sunny-side up quail egg—to be decadently delicious. Proteins are practically flawless; on our visit, a duo of wagyu flat iron steak and red wine-braised short ribs was boldly flavorful, while a cornucopia of haricot verts, cauliflower puree, dried apricots and almonds jazzed up our pan-roasted branzino.

CLEAN BITES

- The restaurant has been awarded a Michelin star.

HUCKLEBERRY

1014 Wilshire Blvd.
310-451-2311

huckleberrycafe.com
@huckcafe

Cuisine:
American (Casual)

Neighborhood:
Santa Monica

Meals Served:
Breakfast, Brunch,
Lunch, Dinner

Farm-fresh, wholesome and charmingly old fashioned, Huckleberry is like a small-town cafe that just happens to be in one of the hippest urban neighborhoods on the planet. Pastry chef Zoe Nathan (who, along with chef-hubby Josh Loeb, also runs Rustic Canyon [p. 148] and Milo & Olive [p. 133]) is responsible for the tempting array of breads and pastries.

Luckily, the deli case of prepared salads, from raw kale to stone fruit, is equally enticing. Order a trio of salads to taste what's fresh at that week's farmers market. Deli meats are all antibiotic- and hormone-free, and rustic sandwich choices include free-range turkey, line-caught tuna salad and Niman Ranch pastrami, all served with mixed greens—antioxidants, please.

Breakfast brings organic egg dishes, while organic rotisserie chicken with wild arugula or roasted potatoes is a hearty choice for dinner. A stone's throw from the beach, this is also a great place to procure picnic provisions.

CLEAN BITES

- Must try: Do you like green eggs and ham? Try Huckleberry's version with La Quercia prosciutto and pesto.
- Even the tofu and flour are organic.
- Love the food? Check out the cookbook: *Huckleberry: Stories, Secrets, and Recipes From Our Kitchen.*

Cuisine:
American (Traditional),
Seafood

Neighborhood:
Hollywood, Santa
Monica

Meals Served:
Brunch (Hollywood),
Lunch, Dinner

THE HUNGRY CAT

1535 N. Vine St.
323-462-2155

thehungrycat.com
@thehungrycat

100 W. Channel Rd.
310-459-3337

Hungry cats are motivated by two things: curiosity and fish. If either of those cravings describe you, then this contemporary seafood-driven bistro will surely satisfy. The vibe is sleek and swank, while the kitchen is all about artisanal craftsmanship.

Despite the fruits-de-mer theme, it's much more than a seafood house; it's a restaurant on the vanguard of inventive, produce-conscious California fare. Dishes fluctuate depending on the freshest catches and ripest market offerings.

You might start your night at the raw bar, in which case try the hamachi with shiso and seasonal fruit if it's available. But the cooked dishes are worth moving into the dining room for. On our visit, we devoured the pure-tasting, elegantly presented king crab legs. A flawless California black cod melted in our mouth. Be sure to add one of the veggie plates to your meal, like roasted beet salad in cumin vinaigrette.

CLEAN BITES

- The restaurant does all of its smoking, curing and pickling in-house.

IL GRANO

11359 Santa Monica Blvd.   ilgrano.com
310-477-7886   @IlGrano

Cuisine:
Italian

Neighborhood:
West LA

Meals Served:
Lunch, Dinner

On an unassuming stretch of Santa Monica Boulevard in West LA, Il Grano turns out one of the finest contemporary Italian meals in the city. The dining room, with its white, black and cream color scheme, is simple yet elegant, just like the creations of chef Salvatore Marino.

Garden-fresh produce and wild-caught seafood are absolute highlights here. To start, try the assortment of daily crudo—our swordfish carpaccio was of divine quality and accompanied by tiny, tangy tomatoes. Another house favorite is the homemade squid ink pasta served al dente with a splash of briny flavor from Santa Barbara sea urchin sauce.

Seafood shines in the entrées, too. If you spot the halibut, order it; it's one of the most delicate, flavorful pieces of fish we've encountered. But non-fish eaters, not to fear—there are also poultry and meat dishes on offer. Adventurous palates: Try the chef's nine-course tasting menu.

CLEAN BITES

- The menu changes monthly to take advantage of organic, seasonal produce and wild, line-caught fish.
- Marino harvests produce from his own garden; his tomato tasting menu (available on Wednesdays during summer) is legendary.
- A vegetarian tasting menu and vegan and gluten-free menus are available.

Cuisine:
Japanese, Macrobiotic

Neighborhood:
Fairfax

Meals Served:
Lunch, Dinner

INAKA

131 S. La Brea Ave.
323-936-9353

inakanaturalfoods.
wordpress.com

Get your yin and yang in harmony at this macrobiotic mainstay, which has been serving up balanced plates of seasonal vegetables, grains and organic seafood for nearly 40 years. The modern space is simple yet elegant, with large round paper lanterns and stark white walls. The home-style Japanese fare is equally so.

You might start with one of the made-fresh-daily soups, like the divinely thick kabocha (pumpkin), or a crisp mixed-green salad with delightful sesame dressing. Vegetable plates include traditional Japanese produce like lotus, burdock and hijiki—a great way to get your daily dose of sea veggies and fermented foods. For something heartier, try the yakisoba (soba or udon studded with cabbage and carrots) or a nourishing seafood hotpot with salmon and sea bass.

The kitchen purposefully goes easy on the seasoning (a hallmark of macrobiotic cooking), but organic soy sauce and ground sesame, as well as basic sea salt and pepper, on each table let you doctor your spice level to satisfaction.

CLEAN BITES

- Must try: The Inaka Plate is a sampling of vegetables, beans and brown rice perfectly calibrated for macrobiotic balance.
- Unfamiliar with traditional Japanese veggies? Check out Inaka's website for a brief tutorial.

JOE'S

1023 Abbot Kinney Blvd.
310-399-5811

joesrestaurant.com
@JoesRestaurant

Cuisine:
Californian, French

Neighborhood:
Venice

Meals Served:
Brunch, Lunch, Dinner

$$$

Don't be fooled by the name—there's nothing average about this Joe. Executive chef and owner Joe Miller has a knack for combining seemingly disparate influences to spectacular effect.

His mix of formal French techniques with Asian and California-influenced aesthetics, as well as his mash-up of fine-dining sensibility with a laidback Venice ethos, has made his eponymous restaurant a sought-after reservation since 1991.

Guided by what's fresh at the local farmers market, the menu changes daily. But expect to find earthy salads—like the sweet-smoky combo of kale, Asian pears and cana de cabra cheese we enjoyed on our visit—as well as abundant fish dishes (we adored the refreshing tuna tartare and house-smoked salmon with cucumbers and lemon oil).

Our porcini mushroom ravioli with savory Parmesan broth and slow-roasted Jidori chicken with seasonal vegetables both proved excellent.

CLEAN BITES

- Besides frequenting local farmers markets, Miller searches out regional items and trends from around the world to influence his creations.
- Try the seven-course tasting menu for a sampling of Joe's best work.
- Every Wednesday night features a Farmers Market dinner series.

Cuisine:
American (Traditional)

Neighborhood:
Santa Monica

Meals Served:
Lunch (Next Door by
Josie), Dinner

JOSIE

2424 Pico Blvd.
310-581-9888

josierestaurant.com
@josierestaurant

NEXT DOOR BY JOSIE

2420 Pico Blvd.
310-581-4201

nextdoorbyjosie.com
@nextdoorbyjosie

Chef Josie Le Balch's eponymous restaurant balances fine-dining elegance with down-to-earth attitude at both her upscale Josie as well as her casual Next Door by Josie.

At Josie, the olive-and-cream front dining room features nods to agricultural abundance, like rosemary centerpieces and banquettes patterned with artichokes. On the plate, that abundance is apparent in the profusion of local produce guiding the French- and Italian-inflected American menu.

Our jaw dropped at straightforward yet deeply flavorful dishes like the jewel tomato tart (a rainbow of tomatoes adorning a smear of creamy goat cheese on a pâte brisée crust) and the whole, boneless "campfire" trout prepared with Blue Lake green beans and citrusy lemongrass nage. Presentations are alluring, from the colorful salads to the tagines served in terracotta-hued earthenware pots.

In addition to treating yourself to a night at Josie, we recommend taking advantage of happy hour and some upscale attention to small plates at Next Door by Josie.

CLEAN BITES

- The hazelnuts are sourced from an organic farm in Oregon.
- The wild rice is hand-harvested from a lake that has never been touched by a motorboat.

JULIANO'S RAW

8951 Santa Monica Blvd.
310-288-0989

planetraw.com
@PlanetRaw

Cuisine:
Raw, Vegetarian/Vegan

Neighborhood:
West Hollywood

Meals Served:
Breakfast, Lunch,
Dinner

When it comes to restaurants for special diets, Juliano's is hardcore. Not only is the cuisine gluten-free, 100% raw and mostly vegan (they use honey), it is also free of ingredients with starchy sugars, including beans, bananas, dates and the like. That's good news for those watching their sugar intake even from natural sources.

So, you can pretty much bet on a completely guilt-free meal at this sleek yet casual cafe. Chef Juliano Brotman, a pioneer of the raw food movement, cooks up imaginative, meatless versions of California favorites including sushi, pasta, burgers and salads. He's practically a magician with his approximations.

In the "cheezy kelp" pasta, he turns cashews and macadamias into a velvety sauce that rivals any cream-based version. Bountiful salads are a highlight, as are the desserts, sweetened only with raw organic honey.

CLEAN BITES

- The cafe doubles as a juice, smoothie and elixir bar.
- You can learn to be a raw foods chef at Raw University, taught by Brotman.
- Every ingredient is non-GMO.

Cuisine:
Vegan/Vegetarian

Neighborhood:
Highland Park

Meals Served:
Breakfast, Lunch

KITCHEN MOUSE

5904 N. Figueroa St.   kitchenmousela.com
323-259-9555

Kitchen Mouse may be located on a sleepy stretch of Figueroa, but the only thing tired about this place is the staff once the lunch slam ends.

The cafe is new, so we had to pardon the appearance (seating was limited, although outdoor tables are soon to come; there was no air conditioning and no exterior signage), but the staff is diligent and friendly and if the locals are willing to give pardon ("The food is totally worth it!" one couple exclaimed on our way out), so are we.

The mushroom and brown rice "sausage" patties were delicious, and the gluten-free pancakes with berries and coconut stole the show—they were light, nutty and not overly sweet.

The dill quinoa salad with arugula, red cabbage and dill pesto was a bit bitter but tempered by a beet tahini slaw. The buffalo bowl, with rice, beans, yams and collard greens, packed in the nutrients but not so much flavor—although the dill, cashew and buffalo sauce gave a welcomed boost.

While there are still some tweaks to be made, thanks to Kitchen Mouse's nutrient-rich, thoughtfully sourced ingredients, we were happy to nibble our way through the menu.

CLEAN BITES

- The kitchen exclusively uses olive oil and sea salt.

KREATION KAFE

1023 Montana Ave.
310-458-4880

kreationkafe.net
@kreationjuice

1202 Abbot Kinney Blvd.
310-314-7778

Cuisine:
American (Casual)

Neighborhood: Santa
Monica, Venice

Meals Served:
Breakfast, Brunch,
Lunch, Dinner

This Persian cafe-cum-juice bar is a "fertile crescent" of organic fare. At the Montana Avenue location you might feel like you've entered an earthly Garden of Eden: the walls are lined with photos of plant life, and smells of fruit waft through the air as produce is blended into build-your-own juices and smoothies.

As for the food, we're keen on the tapas—especially the light, creamy, homemade hummus, which pairs well with the flavorful tabouleh, a citrusy, peppery mix of bulgar, tomato and parsley. The grilled zucchini is perfectly soft on the inside while crispy on the outside.

A selection of kebabs is proffered either as sandwiches on a toasted baguette or as an entrée plate with roasted tomato, whole wheat lavash and a house salad. The free-range chicken kebab comes with abundant grilled bell pepper and onion, making for a messy yet entirely enjoyable sandwich.

CLEAN BITES

- If you like the juices, check out sister enterprise Kreation Juice, with multiple locations (and a juice truck!) across LA.
- The produce, culled from local farmers, is 100% certified organic.
- Part of Kreation Kafe's mission is to inform the community about the healing power of traditional Persian cuisine.

Cuisine:
American (Casual),
Belgian

Meals Served:
Breakfast, Lunch,
Dinner (some
locations)

LE PAIN QUOTIDIEN

Multiple locations

lepainquotidien.com
@LPQLA

The name of this health-conscious, Euro-inspired chain of cafes translates from French as "daily bread," so it's unsurprising that rustic loaves are the main attraction. Organic, stone-ground flour is the foundation for the bread, which becomes a canvas for an array of Belgian-style tartines. Curried chicken with tangy harissa-cranberry chutney is one of our favorites.

But wheat-avoiders: Don't despair. There's room at the cafe's signature wooden communal table for you, too! The wheat-averse can enjoy gluten-free sandwich options; fresh salads such as the quinoa taboulé with chickpeas, avocado, arugula and basil vinaigrette; and baked items like the six-vegetable tart with a buckwheat crust.

At breakfast, staples like steel-cut oatmeal with fresh-picked berries and granola with yogurt provide healthful alternatives to sugary pastries. Freshly brewed organic coffee drinks (with organic milk and agave if you so choose) make for a wholesome start to the day.

CLEAN BITES

- The natural yeast starters used for the bread result in loaves with higher mineral and vitamin content and lower carbohydrate content.
- The centerpiece communal tables are made from reclaimed wood—impressive for such a large chain.
- Many locations offer baking and cooking classes.

LIFEFOOD ORGANIC

1507 Cahuenga Blvd.　　lifefoodorganic.com
323-466-0927　　　　　@LifeFoodOrganic

306 Pico Blvd.
310-450-9693

Cuisine:
Raw, Vegetarian/Vegan

Neighborhood:
Hollywood, Santa
Monica

Meals Served:
Breakfast, Lunch,
Dinner

LifeFood Organic was founded on the principle that raw food (nothing heated above 118 degrees) heals and nourishes the body with its storehouse of enzymes. The small cafe's grab-and-go format makes it easy to live the raw lifestyle, with vegetarian, organic prepared foods and customized fresh juices, smoothies and nut milks.

Everything we tried from the juice bar was distinctive and satisfying. The apple-ginger-lemon juice proved refreshing and crisp, and the especially delicious rainforest smoothie featured a hefty blend of acai, goji and cashews without being too thick. The tart green juice takes its emerald hue from kale, cucumber, celery and green apple.

Although the sushi was a bit bland, our forks battled for the taquitos, composed of seeds, walnuts, almond pulp and sun-dried tomatoes and wrapped in a tasty tortilla made of tamari, coconut meat and lemon. Seaweed salad, another standout, combines arame, hijiki and kale with tahini-miso dressing. Raw-some!

CLEAN BITES

- The organic fare is free of refined sugar, hydrogenated oils, trans fats, GMOs and pesticides.
- LifeFood uses biodegradable packaging whenever possible and recyclable plastics whenever plastic must be used.
- The water is filtered through a nine-stage filtration system.

Cuisine:
Californian

Meals Served:
Breakfast, Lunch,
Dinner

LOCALI

Multiple locations

localiyours.com
@locali

Picture 7-Eleven gone all-natural and you've got Locali: a quick-stop convenience store for the conscious consumer that stocks grab-and-go organic bottled beverages and snacks. The shop has a little gourmet Subway to it, too, with made-to-order sandwiches and salads available at the deli counter.

Overall, the cold sandwiches aren't groundbreaking, but the clean combination of fresh, organic meats, cheeses and vegetables (vegan options abound) proves satisfying. We're partial to the hot paninis, especially the Wayward Pilgrim, with an amalgamation of turkey, Swiss cheese, crushed walnuts, spinach, raspberry jam and Dijon on six-grain bread that delivers a savory twist on Thanksgiving flavors.

Salad-wise, the Boss' KO Kale is worth a try. The kale is massaged with olive oil, lemon and sea salt, then served either "naughty" (with sun-dried tomatoes, walnuts and cayenne) or "nice" (with cranberries, walnuts and agave). For a sweet finish and healthy digestion boost, slurp one of the tasty probiotic smoothies.

CLEAN BITES

- Sandwich meats are free of antibiotics, hormones, fillers, gluten and casein; vegan meats are non-GMO—a rarity for a deli.
- Locali uses four-stage, reverse-osmosis filtered water in its food prep, ice, smoothies and coffee.

LUCQUES

8474 Melrose Ave.
323-655-6277

lucques.com
@LucquesLA

Cuisine:
Californian,
Mediterranean

Neighborhood:
West Hollywood

Meals Served:
Lunch, Dinner

Ensconced in an ivy-covered carriage house, Lucques is an iconic LA dining destination from local celeb chef Suzanne Goin (A.O.C. [p. 70], the Hungry Cat [p. 114]). Get cozy with a date by the brick fireplace in the elegant dining room, or soften your power lunch by dining amongst the lush vine-enveloped walls framing the patio.

Goin has an uncanny knack for achieving sublime results with simple ingredients—and without trendy techniques or fussy sauces. Her French-Mediterranean fare is rendered through a California lens, and every dish is enhanced by the freshness and quality of the produce and proteins she sources.

Since the menu changes seasonally, there's always something different on offer. But some of our favorite dishes are mainstays. Definitely try the clean-your-plate delicious ricotta dumplings with market vegetables and fall-off-the-bone tender braised beef short ribs. Don't miss Goin's famous Sunday Suppers, which offer a taste of what's freshest at the market.

CLEAN BITES

- The starter of lucques olives (from which the restaurant takes its name) and almonds is a delicious, healthy alternative to bread and butter.
- Want to master Goin's market-to-table cooking style? Check out her book *Sunday Suppers at Lucques*.

LYFE KITCHEN

9540 Washington Blvd.
310-507-7955

lyfekitchen.com
@LYFEkitchen

Cuisine:
American (Casual)

Neighborhood:
Culver City

Meals Served:
Breakfast, Lunch,
Dinner

With its diverse menu and mix-and-match protein choices, Lyfe Kitchen has mastered the art of options. The approachable menu runs the gamut from mahi fish tacos to Thai-inspired rice bowls, and protein options—chicken breast, soy-based "chick'n" (we recommend steering clear of this one), salmon and tofu—can be tailored to many of the dishes. Even the large, sunny warehouse-style space fits to your dining mood, with couches, bar stools, communal tables and outdoor tables.

Start hearty with a Buffalo wing appetizer that's baked instead of fried, or go lighter with grilled artichokes so tender that all they need is a squeeze of lemon. Burgers come at every speed: grass-fed beef with cheddar, breaded chicken with chipotle aioli, or a veggie patty (we recommend steering clear of the Daiya cheese). A chicken and mushroom whole-wheat penne is topped with surprisingly creamy cashew sauce. For an Asian-inspired flavor, barramundi gets a spicy lift from a pungent kimchi broth.

With this many healthy-minded options in one menu, Lyfe Kitchen has something to fit whatever mood you're in—plus, it's a great go-to place for eating with a picky crowd.

CLEAN BITES

- If you have dietary restrictions, log onto the website to filter Lyfe Kitchen's menu by gluten-free, seasonal and vegan options.
- Each dish has fewer than 600 calories.

M CAFÉ DE CHAYA

Multiple locations   mcafedechaya.com
@WeLoveMCafe

Cuisine:
Californian, Japanese,
Macrobiotic

Meals Served:
Breakfast, Brunch,
Lunch, Dinner

Just like its more formal sister restaurant, Chaya (p. 83), M Café balances Japanese culinary influences with a European aesthetic, but with a more deli-meets-patisserie vibe. The "M" here hints at the restaurant's macrobiotic leanings, which emphasize whole grains and vegetables with a smattering of fresh seafood.

The Asian-inspired dishes run the gamut from sushi to bento boxes to udon noodle bowls. We especially dig the light, vegetarian bi bim bop with a side of fiery kimchi. Salads, sandwiches, and burgers are also represented. The Big Macro, a flavorful vegetable patty on a wholesome house-baked bun with sprouts is a tasty alternative to the gluttonous fast-food burger it's playfully named after. Sweet and savory breakfasts round out the eclectic menu.

When ordering at the busy counter, you'll undeniably be tempted by the display case of desserts like fruit tarts and tiramisu. Go ahead: indulge! They're made with no eggs, dairy or refined sugar.

CLEAN BITES

- Must try: organic miso soup.
- There are abundant gluten-free options on the menu, including Babycakes' gluten-free pastries (see p. 167).
- The kitchen uses organic tempeh and tofu—a rarity in many Asian restaurants.

Cuisine:
American
(Contemporary)

Neighborhood:
Malibu

Meals Served:
Breakfast, Lunch,
Dinner

MALIBU FARM

23000 Pacific Coast Hwy.   malibu-farm.com
310-456-1112   @Malibufarm

Perched at the end of the historic Malibu Beach Pier with picturesque views and prime beach crowds, Malibu Farm could have opted for the standard beach boardwalk fare. Instead, it elevated beach shack food to a whole new level.

The airy, farmhouse-chic restaurant sources produce from organic farms and turns out seasonally minded plates that all seem to be better than the one before. Chopped salad piled high with cubes of beets and butternut squash, colorful coconut and vegetable curry and lightly breaded, silver dollar-size Dungeness crab cakes all tasted perfectly balanced, satisfying and unbelievably fresh.

Brunch crowds sip local Caffe Luxxe coffee while digging into Swedish pancakes or fluffy scrambled eggs with fresh ricotta and smoked salmon. Perennial beach favorites like burgers get a tasty upgrade here—grass-fed beef with pepperoncini aioli, or a meaty portobello burger with heirloom tomato slices. Be sure to check out the sun deck for expansive views of the legendary Malibu waves that break just off the pier.

CLEAN BITES

- Must try: the vegan coconut dish with tofu and veggies.
- The cafe started as a pop-up restaurant when chef and owner Helene Henderson, who keeps a 2-acre organic farm at her Malibu home, started cooking farm-to-table meals for friends.
- Check out the local-only retail products, with Malibu-centric items such as honey, olive oil and jam.

MB POST

1142 Manhattan Ave.
310-545-5405

eatmbpost.com
@ChefDLeFevre

Cuisine:
American (Casual)

Neighborhood:
Manhattan Beach

Meals Served:
Brunch, Dinner

Set in a former post office, MB Post has the sophisticated small-plates concept signed, sealed and delivered. Old fashioned steel mailboxes and iron grid windows nod to the space's postal past, while expansive communal tables, shareable dishes and handcrafted cocktails add up to a buzzing "social house" scene.

The seasonally fluctuating menu cruises effortlessly from the Far East to South America to the Mediterranean. Veggies are a main attraction, not just side-dish afterthoughts. We savored the blistered Blue Lake green beans bathed in fiery chili sauce and a simply dressed Tuscan kale and quinoa salad.

Not surprisingly, given the beach-adjacent location and chef David LeFevre's seafood expertise (he formerly cooked at downtown's Water Grill [see p. 165]), fish dishes here truly shine. Selections change based on availability, but our favorite plate was the moist steelhead trout resting in soft, lemony leeks. Compassionately sourced meat dishes like buttery skirt steak will please discerning carnivores.

CLEAN BITES

- The restaurant sources most of its meats from the Meyer Farm "Never Ever" program. Sick animals are never slaughtered, and hormones and antibiotics are never used.
- The menu changes so often that sometimes hand-written notes will accompany it, helping to curate that evening's selections.

Cuisine:
French

Neighborhood:
Santa Monica

Meals Served:
Dinner

MÉLISSE

1104 Wilshire Blvd.
310-395-0881

melisse.com
@josiahcitrin

Dining at Mélisse should be on every foodie's bucket list. Chef Josiah Citrin's contemporary French gastronomy has earned prestigious international accolades, and for good reason. This is cuisine as art and theater: Waitstaff in dapper three-piece suits circulate through the elegant purple-walled dining room announcing each beautifully plated dish upon its arrival at your table.

But the food would be noteworthy without such fanfare. We're keen on the fact that seasonal, local produce, not cream and butter, guides the chef's opus. Offerings shift frequently depending upon what's fresh at the market, but expect twists on French classics, such as vegetarian cassoulet with portobello mushrooms and shelling beans, or almond-crusted Dover sole accompanied by corn and chanterelles in brown butter.

The elaborate tasting menus are pretty structured but can be customized. If you can resist the decadent caviar and "fromage" selections, Mélisse will be one of your finest healthy meals.

CLEAN BITES

- Must try: Date-night couples should consider ordering the rotisserie chicken stuffed with truffles for two.
- Citrin hand-picks produce from the Santa Monica Farmers Market and hosts a bi-annual dinner to honor local growers.
- Check out the all-vegetarian tasting menu.

MENDOCINO FARMS

Multiple locations

mendocinofarms.com
@MendocinoFarms

Cuisine:
American (Casual)

Meals Served:
Lunch, Dinner (at
some locations)

This "eco-artisan" sandwich chain combines farm-fresh ingredients with a gourmet sensibility and then puts it all between two slices of bread. The result is impeccably crafted, innovative sandwiches that are well worth braving the long lunch lines for.

Case in point: the chicken MBT, an Italian-inspired amalgamation of thick, roasted chicken breast slices, local creamy Gioia mozzarella, pesto, tomato and mixed greens on ciabatta. Delizioso!

But if neither meat nor bread are your thing, no worries. Gluten-avoiders can have their sandwich on Rising Heart Bakery's gluten-free bread, and vegans have several tasty options, most notably the vegan shawarma—a hefty whole-wheat wrap filled with faux shawarma (made from chickpeas, not processed soy), vegan tzatziki and Greek salad fixings.

Salads layered with veggies, proteins and crunchy additions like the house-made honey-roasted almonds are equally well executed, but sandwiches are what bring most of the crowds through the door.

CLEAN BITES

- The restaurant takes its name and inspiration from Mendocino County, which is known for its sustainable farming and support of the slow food movement.
- Want a healthier bread choice? Swap your ciabatta for buckwheat or seeded whole wheat.

MICHAEL'S

1147 3rd St.
310-451-0843

michaelssantamonica.com
@msantamonica

In 1979, Michael McCarty helped define modern American cooking when he opened his namesake restaurant. Today, Michael's farmers market-driven approach to contemporary cuisine is steadfast, but a 2012 re-do of the space and menu spruced things up for a more casual, smartphone-savvy clientele.

Gone are the white tablecloths and formal serving ware; in are moderately priced small plates served on Instagram-friendly wooden boards. The lush patio remains the main dining space, but the candlelit lounge, with its all-night happy hour, is hopping too.

While pizza and taco selections reflect the laid-back approach, the kitchen retains its fine-dining sensibility. Insanely good beef sliders, for example, are made with grass-fed wagyu and topped with tasty white cheddar, crispy shallots and Russian dressing.

The kitchen falters with trendy dishes like the Asian-style lamb chops. But classics like wild bass on a bed of market vegetables showcase the refinement that put Michael's on the map.

CLEAN BITES

- Must try: Michael's burger.
- The seasonal menu is full of whatever happens to be freshest at the Santa Monica Farmers Market in a given week (check the list of farms on the menu).
- McCarty can often be seen circulating among tables, and his modern art collection graces the walls.

MILO & OLIVE

2723 Wilshire Blvd.
310-453-6776

miloandolive.com
@MiloandOlive

Cuisine:
Italian

Neighborhood:
Santa Monica

Meals Served:
Breakfast, Lunch,
Dinner

To call this diminutive dining room a pizza joint would be grossly reductionist, and yet, in this addition to husband-wife team Josh Loeb and Zoe Nathan's collection of restaurants (Rustic Canyon [p. 148], Huckleberry [p. 113]), pizzas are indeed the main focus.

The ultra-thin-crust pizzas with chunky edges and seasonal toppings are almost too generously sized (enough for two to share) for the amount of tabletop you've got at your disposal. Since there are just eight counter seats and two eight-seat communal tables, competition for chairs—and elbow room—is at a premium.

The Italian-themed menu is rounded out by seasonal small plates and pastas. Try the succulent free-range chicken meatballs (our favorite dish) and flawless ricotta gnocchi robed in tomato sauce.

Fresh salads are also abundant. It's the kind of place where farmers market eco-warriors and diehard pizza fanatics will be equally pleased—as long as they can all find a seat.

CLEAN BITES

- Zoe Nathan's artisan breads are available from the bakery.
- The restaurant uses locally made mozzarella.

THE MISFIT

225 Santa Monica Blvd.
310-656-9800

themisfitbar.com
@TheMisfitSaMo

Cuisine:
American (Casual),
Gastropub

Neighborhood:
Santa Monica

Meals Served:
Brunch, Lunch, Dinner

With its focus on farm-to-table fare, The Misfit is definitely an oddball in the typical bar food department. No wings or sliders in sight: This uncommonly good and good-for-you restaurant-bar serves up produce-driven small plates, grass-fed burgers and bistro specialties.

On the other hand, The Misfit fits in perfectly with its expansive, chic space, where design details like safe deposit boxes and antique tin ceiling tiles recall the building's former use as a bank. Mirrored columns, globe fixtures and shelves of books impart an erudite mystique.

Seasonal availability dictates what's on offer, but if you see the Brussels sprouts salad, grab it. The bitterness of the sprouts is cleverly offset by the earthy sweetness of dried blueberries and saltiness of manchego. The Misfit burger—dripping with Dijon, cheddar and caramelized onions—is hard to pass up. But with plenty of meatless choices, vegetarians won't have to feel like misfits.

CLEAN BITES

- The restaurant is happy to accommodate vegan, vegetarian and gluten-free diners. Don't see something for you on the menu? Just ask.
- Experience chef Dom Ruggiero's creations on the cheap: The Barfly Lunch features a different dish each day of the week for only $5! Rules? You must be sitting at the bar, and get your order in by 4 p.m.

MIXT GREENS

350 S. Grand Ave.
213-290-2572

mixtgreens.com
@mixtgreens

5757 Wilshire Blvd.
213-290-3718

Cuisine:
American (Casual)

Neighborhood:
Downtown, Mid-Wilshire

Meals Served: Lunch,
Dinner (Mid-Wilshire)

With the catchphrase "Lettuce rock your world," fast-casual salad spot Mixt Greens is at once health conscious and hip to the environmental scene, a combo it dubs "eco-gourmet."

Local greens and veggies from organic, sustainable suppliers are the inspiration for an array of salads that range from classic Cobbs and Caesars to distinct creations like the refreshing Maui salad, with butter lettuce, coriander-crusted seared ahi tuna, mango-citrus vinaigrette and crushed macadamia nuts. Seasonal specials exploit produce at its peak.

Or, get creative with the design-your-own option—choose from a cornucopia of greens, proteins, veggies, cheeses, nuts and gluten-free dressings. Every item is presented before you salad-bar style, so you can see just how fresh every ingredient is.

Salads are clearly the rock stars of this operation, but the sandwiches (served with a heaping portion of leafy greens) are incredibly tasty, too.

CLEAN BITES

- Check out the *Mixt Greens Cookbook*.
- Packaging and take-away containers are 100% compostable, and the restaurant achieves 85% waste reduction through composting and recycling. All locations are built with renewable, recycled and environmentally friendly materials.
- Mixt Greens contributes to many organizations including Slow Food USA and the Business Council on Climate Change.

MOHAWK BEND

2141 W. Sunset Blvd.
213-483-2337

mohawk.la
@mohawkla

At this high-energy restaurant/bar housed in a former vaudeville theater, the scene is pure Echo Park. Droves of hipsters pile in for craft beers—72 on tap—and comfort eats.

In catering to the cool kids, the kitchen has struck just the right balance between a serious commitment to eco-consciousness and craft (they use only California ingredients and have dedicated vegan and non-vegan prep areas) and a lighthearted concession to novelty (they update pub food with healthy twists).

Bar classics get a vegan makeover, with pizza, burgers and bar snacks such as Buffalo wings re-imagined as vehicles for showcasing veggies. (The Buffalo "wings" are actually cauliflower—a nice break from the ubiquitous fried seitan.) Among the hearty salads, we're partial to the Flash Gordon, which takes its clever name from flash-grilled Little Gem lettuce paired with citrus segments and avocado. Meat eater? Enjoy meaty treats like the house-made Italian sausage on the Abe Froman pizza or a beef burger.

CLEAN BITES

- Brick-oven pizzas are made with organic California flour and sauce from 100% organic California tomatoes and herbs.
- All menu items are vegan unless marked (NV) and the kitchen has a designated prep station for vegan fare.
- The drink menu pays homage to local, small-scale breweries, wineries and distilleries.

MUDDY LEEK

8631 Washington Blvd.
310-838-2281

muddyleek.com
@MuddyLeek

Cuisine:
American
(Contemporary)

Neighborhood:
Culver City

Meals Served:
Lunch, Dinner

A block from the bustling restaurants at Helm's Bakery, Whitney Flood's Muddy Leek is an elegant retreat with a refined attitude. The space is modern and clean, and so is the food. The menu is progressive (goat, anyone?) and sustainable. Everything is prepared in-house, from the warm bread that opens your meal to the divine dark chocolate truffles that finish it.

Driven by seasonal cooking, the menu changes frequently. Fire-roasted shrimp with grits and kale was a delicious starter, but the standout was the zucchini linguine served with basil brown butter and a poached egg. You may never yearn for wheat noodles again. Bronzed king salmon was served with a tangy, creamy cucumber salad and garbanzo blini. The grass-fed beef cheeks were tender, but you may want to ask for it medium-rare, as ours was a bit overcooked for our taste. The potato lasagna was perfect.

The staff is justifiably proud of the food, and the service reflects this.

CLEAN BITES

- Muddy Leek uses only non-GMO rice bran oil for frying and sautéeing, and extra-virgin olive oil for dressings and seasoning.
- The restaurant recycles everything that can be re-used, including the cooking oil. It buys quick-breakdown trash bags, and it composts every bit of food it can.
- Water filtration is a two-stage system, and all the water left in the glasses is saved and used for watering plants.

NATIVE FOODS CAFÉ

Multiple locations

nativefoods.com
@nativefoodscafe

Cuisine:
Vegetarian/Vegan

Meals Served:
Lunch, Dinner

While the term "vegan chain restaurant" may seem like an oxymoron, Native Foods Café has proved that demand for tasty, animal-free fare is expanding. The vibe is laid-back and informal, but the restaurant doesn't take its cuisine casually. Everything, including the plant-based proteins and nut cheese, is made in-house, from scratch.

The globally inspired menu includes salads, bowls, wraps and burgers. Asian-themed dishes like the Saigon roll (lemon grass tofu, veggies and rice with zippy peanut sauce) are among the most flavorful, and the bowl creations travel the map from Thailand to Greece to Morocco.

But there are also meatless twists on American classics. Our favorite is the scorpion burger, a blackened tempeh burger with hot chipotle sauce, a refreshing crunch from romaine and carrot, and tasty texture from avocado and caramelized onions, served with herbed sweet-potato fries.

CLEAN BITES

- The restaurant serves organic tempeh and tofu.
- Soy-free, gluten-free and nut-free menus are available upon request.
- Native Community Days are held twice a month—desserts are free and a portion of the sales are donated to community organizations.

NINETHIRTY

930 Hilgard Ave.
310-208-8765

ninethirtyw.com
@NineThirtyW

Cuisine:
American
(Contemporary)

Neighborhood:
Westwood

Meals Served:
Breakfast, Dinner

You don't need to be a tourist to justify coming to the W Hotel in Westwood for a meal at NineThirty. It's a stylish boîte where the produce is local, and some of the guests are, too.

Chef Dakota Weiss catapults the fare beyond typically bland hotel grub with an eclectic, innovative menu grounded in seasonal, sustainable ingredients.

An assortment of "social bites" and "beginning plates" is robust enough to make an informal meal at the communal table. We'd order the white corn bisque with queso fresco and whatever market-fresh salad happens to be in rotation, like the butter lettuce salad we enjoyed with blackberries and goat cheese.

Or, hunker down for one of the larger plates amid the dining room's metallic fixtures and velvet drapes. Portions are generous, and selections range from fresh fish to beef bourguignon to a vegetarian market-inspired dish.

CLEAN BITES

- Chef Dakota Weiss was a former Top Chef: Texas contestant.
- NineThirty is routinely named one of the best hotel restaurants by Eater LA.

Cuisine:
Italian

Neighborhood:
Hollywood

Meals Served:
Lunch, Dinner

OSTERIA LA BUCA

5210 Melrose Ave.
323-462-1900

osterialabuca.com
@OsteriaLaBucaLA

Osteria La Buca is on to a good thing. With an airy, lively space constructed from sustainable materials, an open kitchen, outstanding staff and some of the best Italian fare around, this neighborhood tavern has it all.

Start with the locally sourced, ricotta-filled, melt-in-your-mouth squash blossoms and the crispy Brussels sprouts, topped with a poached organic egg, breadcrumbs and tangy anchovy vinaigrette, before moving on to the house-made, out-of-this-world pasta options. The short rib ravioli was a stand out—luscious pockets of pasta surround tender beef enhanced by a simple cream sauce. Gluten-adverse? Don't fret, gluten-free varieties are available.

Go a bit lighter with sustainably sourced proteins such as the Idaho trout and Wednesday's popular special, chicken Diavolo. Both are excellent—distinguished by plentiful portions and served with seasonal vegetables.

CLEAN BITES

- All to-go boxes, paper hand towels, utensils, and toilet paper are made from 100% post-consumer recycled products. Even the ceramic dishes and cleaning supplies have an eco-focus.
- Various "happenings" occur on-site. Check the website to find what's on deck.

PACE

2100 Laurel Canyon Blvd.
323-654-8583

peaceinthecanyon.com
@pacerestaurant

Cuisine:
Italian

Neighborhood:
Laurel Canyon

Meals Served:
Dinner

$$$

This dreamy Italian restaurant captures the hippie music-meets-nature roots of woodsy Laurel Canyon. Eclectic art, brick walls, live jazz and a low-lit patio with canyon breezes add up to a quirky, romantic setting.

The light yet flavorful Italian fare is driven by produce. Chef Sandy Gendel hand-picks the all-organic fruit and veggies from local farmers markets twice a week and, on the menu, name-checks the farms supported.

Start with the vegan soup of the day or the insalata vegetale, a chopped veggie salad with a delicate red wine vinaigrette. Although the pastas are made fresh in-house daily and the pizzas come on ciabatta crust, we'd skip these in favor of the entrées. The cedar wood-grilled salmon is an absolute standout, with fresh herbs and shallots punctuating every bite, and the seasonal veggie sides cooked with Pace's Tuscan organic olive oil make accompaniments so delicious that you'll forget they're healthy.

CLEAN BITES

- Pace encourages community symbiosis by selling the eclectic and vibrant works of local artists.
- Live jazz on Monday nights!

PETTY CASH TAQUERIA

7360 Beverly Blvd.
323-933-5300

pettycashtaqueria.com
@PettyCashLA

Petty Cash Taqueria is a welcome refuge from run-of-the-mill taquerias, offering sustainable and sophisticated fare in a hip setting.

We started with a popular standout, roasted cauliflower nachos. House-made tortilla chips are baked with a sprinkling of kale, tender cauliflower and cheese. The hamachi ceviche was also very good—the fish super-fresh although a bit over-sauced for our taste. Noteworthy were the machacha beef brisket quesadillas, topped with a tasty, cooling, crema.

Tacos are served individually and a la carte. Fillings include beef, pork, shrimp, fish, octopus, crickets (protein, baby!), potatoes and mushrooms. The Baja fish taco was especially tasty—the fish was tender and crispy, lightly dressed with shredded cabbage and pico de gallo. Also delicious was the grilled maitake mushroom taco, an ideal vegan offering.

The service was outstanding. Clearly, the staff is rightfully proud of the food they serve.

CLEAN BITES

- Petty Cash boasts a rooftop garden with 35 aeroponic towers. Some of the produce grown there may end up on your plate!
- The restaurant features hand-painted murals by Los Angeles street artist Retna and graffiti art by some of Petty Cash's kitchen staff.

PONO BURGER

829 Broadway
310-584-7005

ponoburger.com
@PonoBurger

Cuisine:
American (Casual)

Neighborhood:
Santa Monica

Meals Served:
Lunch, Dinner

In Hawaiian, "pono" means "doing things the right way" and for chef/owner Makani Gerardi that means providing the same quality food to her customers as she would her family. Sourcing only from small California family farms, all the meat is organic and from grass-fed cows.

We sampled the Posh, a beef burger with blue cheese, house-made truffle aioli, organic mushrooms and arugula. The meat was lean and those umami-filled toppings were a nice touch. The organic fries (russet and sweet potato) are fried in non-GMO rice bran oil and served with aioli. The russets were the winner; their texture and flavor popped. But the sweet potato fries came with a bacon aioli that was quickly addicting.

Note that because the Hawaiian palette runs sweet, so do the buns and some toppings.

CLEAN BITES

- Sweet tooth? Even the milkshakes here feature organic ingredients. The organic strawberry milkshake featuring Straus Family Creamery soft serve is killer.
- Check the Pono Burger website to learn more about sourcing practices and purveyors.

Cuisine:
Vegetarian/Vegan

Neighborhood:
Mid-Wilshire

Meals Served:
Brunch, Lunch, Dinner

POWERPLANT SUPERFOOD CAFE

5671 W. Pico Blvd.
323-965-2233

powerplantsuperfood
cafe.com

Don't let its tiny size fool you: This unassuming cafe is a powerhouse of nutrient-dense fare. Placards on each of the half-dozen tables inform you of the health benefits of various "superfoods," from berries to coconut. These superstars of the plant world are the foundation of the eatery's organic, plant-based, gluten-free menu.

The eclectic offerings reflect the multiculturalism of LA. We were enamored of the kimchi avocado hummus appetizer made with "super greens" fermented in-house; the Korea-meets-Middle East combo is surprisingly scrumptious. Another favorite is the juicy tempeh Reuben, with house-made organic tempeh, sauerkraut, organic Swiss cheese and cornichon dressing. You won't miss the corned beef.

For the most antioxidants for your buck, try the superfood salad, loaded with greens, ruby beets, carrots and the restaurant's signature superfood nut-seed crumble; the blood orange-fennel-ginger dressing makes a perfect match. Smoothies, sweetened only with dates, pack quite a nutritious, delicious punch, too.

CLEAN BITES

- Gluten-avoiders rejoice! Sandwiches are served on gluten-free Grindstone Bakery quinoa-millet bread, and the pasta is made from red lentils.
- The cafe doubles as a pressed juice, smoothie and organic coffee bar.

THE RABBIT HOLE CAFE

30651 E. Thousand Oaks Blvd.,   rabbitholefoods.com
Unit H
818-889-1554

Cuisine:
American (Casual)

Neighborhood:
Agoura Hills

Meals Served:
Breakfast, Brunch,
Lunch, Dinner

Tucked away in a nondescript strip mall, The Rabbit Hole Cafe is a cozy, neighborhood gem with a flair for whimsy. From its Alice in Wonderland-inspired décor to concoctions like the Frozen French Toast smoothie (whipped up from banana, maca, almond milk and dates), the cafe's friendly atmosphere is matched by an approachable menu of inventive, mostly vegetarian fare.

With more than 20 dishes, there's plenty to satisfy picky dietary restrictions. The only meat comes in the form of a few sandwiches (sustainably-caught yellowfin tuna, organic chicken and turkey) and just about everything can be made vegetarian. Organic smoothies are sweet pick-me-ups creatively blended with natural ingredients like coconut yogurt and cacao nibs.

The baked comfort foods include a surprisingly creamy vegan mushroom stroganoff topped with kale and a hearty mushroom sauce. Slippery glass noodles made from raw kelp get a spicy kick with a tongue-tingling roasted sesame dressing. Daily soups range from potato leek to cheesy Brussels sprouts. With a menu this much fun to get lost in, the cafe name begins to make perfect sense.

CLEAN BITES

- Must try: the Rabbit Hole Bowl, a generous helping of quinoa, brown rice and sweet potatoes layered on a bed of crispy fried kale and ginger lemon dressing that loyal customers swear by.
- The menu lists which ingredients are organic and from where they are sourced.

Cuisine:
Macrobiotic,
Vegetarian/Vegan

Meals Served:
Brunch, Lunch, Dinner

REAL FOOD DAILY

Multiple locations

realfood.com
@RealFoodDaily

Real Food Daily (or "RFD," as it's affectionately known) has been "keeping it real" on the plant-based, sustainable tip since 1993—way before veganism and organics were part of the culinary zeitgeist. Founder and green food pioneer Ann Gentry fuses Eastern macrobiotic concepts with California-style seasonal cooking that embraces multicultural influences.

Burgers and sandwiches are menu staples, and Gentry really nails the essentials—satisfying proteins (without relying on heavily processed soy substitutes), tasty nut cheeses and killer dressings. We didn't miss the meat at all in the Total Reuben, with marinated tempeh (using non-GMO whole soy), horseradish cashew cheese, tangy sauerkraut and thousand island dressing on sturdy sprouted rye bread, with no sogginess in sight.

Main courses ranging from lasagna to tacos rotate with the seasons, while bedrock bowls of macrobiotic goodness (beans, brown rice, sea vegetables) are always available. The restaurant's modern decor makes sustainable eating stylish. Carnivores, beware: RFD may convert you to veganism.

CLEAN BITES

- The menu is 100% organic and free of preservatives, pesticides, artificial sweeteners, food dyes, trans-fats, soy-isolates and genetically modified organisms.
- Gentry has authored two cookbooks, *Vegan Family Meals*, *Real Food for Everyone* and *The Real Food Daily Cookbook*.

RESTAURANT AT THE GETTY CENTER

1200 Getty Center Dr.
310-440-6810

getty.edu/visit/center/
eat.html

Cuisine:
American (Traditional),
Seafood

Neighborhood:
Brentwood

Meals Served:
Brunch, Lunch, Dinner

The Getty's great art deserves a creative meal to match, and this upscale restaurant does the job. Set in one of the campus' Richard Meier-designed buildings, the dining room boasts floor-to-ceiling windows overlooking stunning canyon views. It's a posh perch for a leisurely mid-museum lunch break or a romantic sunset dinner.

Employing local produce, the menu changes with the seasons. Lunch and dinner offerings are fairly similar, with traditional appetizer and entrée categories. We found the salads to be among the best items. Our watermelon feta salad was surprisingly spiced up with pickled radishes and jalapeño.

Entrées are protein-heavy, with the bounty of both land and sea represented. On our visit, the standout was the grilled salmon, a buttery fillet served with the skin on and a healthy side of broccoli, cauliflower and spinach. Despite a blunder here and there, the dining experience did justice to the artistic context.

CLEAN BITES

- While lunch is served Tuesday through Saturday, there is dinner service only on Saturdays (as well as Fridays during the summer).
- There's a more casual cafe serving sandwiches, salads and the like on the level below the restaurant.

Cuisine:
American
(Contemporary)

Neighborhood:
Santa Monica

Meals Served:
Dinner

RUSTIC CANYON

1119 Wilshire Blvd.
310-393-7050

rusticcanyonwinebar.com
@RCwinebar

Feel like sitting down to a home-cooked, candlelit dinner among friends? That's the ethos at Rustic Canyon, which got its start when founder Josh Loeb began hosting suppers at his home in the eponymous Santa Monica Mountains enclave. Teamed with his wife Zoe Nathan (the duo also run Huckleberry [p. 113] and Milo & Olive [p. 133]), Loeb has continued the homemade, earthy theme in the farmers market-driven menu.

The emphasis here is on small plates to share, and the healthy portions are indeed shareable. You might start with an order of citrusy green olives followed by inventive fruit and vegetable salads incorporating fresh nuts and cheeses. The menu also features four or five large plates on any given night, including meat and fish options paired with veggie sides.

Thirsty? Rustic Canyon bills itself as a wine bar, so expect an array of global boutique wines along with seasonal cocktails and artisanal beers.

CLEAN BITES

- Check out Rustic Canyon's website to learn more about its suppliers.

SAGE

4130 Sepulveda Blvd.
424-228-5835

sagaveganbistro.com
@SageVegan

1700 W. Sunset Blvd.
213-989-1718

This buzzy vegan bistro hits all the right notes. Responsibly sourced produce? Check. An inventive menu with true culinary merit? Check. An impossibly hip crowd? It goes without saying.

The seasonally shifting menu is a moving target, but the eclectic dishes tend to hop the map from Italy to Thailand to the American heartland. At dinner, you might start with the garlicky, "buttery" Brussels sprouts and squash appetizer with tempeh bacon. Pasta dishes, which might include spinach-basil ravioli and eggplant arrabiata, are as good as any traditional trattoria. (Pizzas are served at the Culver City location.)

At lunch, we're fans of the falafel bowl, which pairs crispy falafel spheres with juicy oranges and tomatoes over moist quinoa. No matter what's in the lineup, we're impressed with the kitchen's versatile range. And save room for dessert: There's an ice cream counter serving raw, vegan frozen treats from KindKreme and fruit smoothies.

CLEAN BITES

- The tofu and tempeh are organic.
- At the Culver City location, enjoy 20% off appetizers, beer and cocktails during happy hour, 4 to 6 p.m. and 10 p.m. to midnight.

Cuisine:
American
(Contemporary)

Neighborhood:
West Hollywood

Meals Served:
Breakfast, Lunch,
Dinner

SALT'S CURE

7494 Santa Monica Blvd.   saltscure.com
323-850-7258   @SaltsCure

At this laidback American eatery, nothing on your plate comes from farther than six hours away (by car). Whole animals and fish are butchered in-house, and everything from mustard to charcuterie is crafted from scratch.

That translates to authentic farm-fresh tastes. Fluctuating daily, the chalkboard menu is mounted at the rear of the small, wood- and brick-paneled dining room. While choices are somewhat limited, every dish is a winner—there's no filler, and nothing's wasted (check out the nose-to-tail cured meats).

Simple preparations allow the pure flavor of each ingredient to shine. A mélange of stone fruits doused in basil vinaigrette over milk curd was one of the most creative, delicious salads we've tasted all year. Succulent blackened half chicken wasn't overwhelmed by the cumin-cinnamon spice mix. Perfectly roasted petite carrots had a dash of flat-leaf parsley, while moist Swiss chard was brightened by diced tomatoes. Even mashed potatoes here taste healthy.

CLEAN BITES

- Must try: the drool-worthy pork chop, which is always on the menu (preparations vary) and is butchered to order.
- Check the restaurant's Facebook page for a photo of the day's dinner menu so you know what's cooking before you arrive.
- Questions about the sourcing? Ask the knowledgeable waiters or the chefs in the open kitchen—they'll gush about the provenance of everything.

SEED KITCHEN

1604 Pacific Ave.
310-396-1604

seedkitchen.com
@seedrestaurants

It's hard to imagine a healthier setup: a vegan, macrobiotic restaurant just a short walk from the bike paths and surf-friendly waves of Venice Beach. Founders Eric Lechasseur and Sanae Suzuki truly walk that walk—they adopted a macrobiotic diet and active, outdoor lifestyle to heal their own health woes.

The casual, quick-service format makes it easy to swing by on your way to the sand. Although the macrobiotic bowls filled with brown rice and sea vegetables aren't anything to write home about, they are a supremely healthful option and the burgers and salads put greasy chains to shame.

Absolutely order the barbecue tempeh burger (with sweet potato fries!)—sticky, smoky vegan "barbecue sauce" livens up hot strips of tempeh and crisp fresh veggies on warm ciabatta.(We recommend steering clear of the seitan in favor of the organic tempeh.) The ume-plum ranch dressing in the enormous "chop-chop" salad is clean-the-bowl delicious. Tacos and paninis also make great, portable choices for a vegan beach picnic.

CLEAN BITES

- Seed offers meditation and cooking classes along with nutritional and herbal counseling (for both you and your pets!).
- Check out Suzuki's book, *Love, Sanae*, for recipes and tips on healing with macrobiotics.

Cuisine:
Japanese, Macrobiotic,
Vegetarian/Vegan

Neighborhood: Culver
City, Downtown

Meals Served:
Dinner

SHOJIN

333 S. Alameda St.,
Suite 310
213-617-0305

theshojin.com
@shojinlove

12406 Washington Blvd.
310-390-0033

There's nothing fishy about the sushi at Shojin—literally. Shojin takes the greatest hits of Japanese cuisine—sushi rolls, tempura, ramen—and gives them a vegan makeover.

Presentations are colorful and creative, and the spicy offerings pack a serious flavor punch. The Dynamite roll explodes from fiery tofu "tuna," spiked vegan mayo and a soy-sesame sauce charged with chili pepper flakes. The slurptastic hot-and-spicy ramen with cabbage, sprouts and scallions had us sweating by the last spoonful. Creamy wasabi mayo gave a potent kick to the crispy shiitake mushroom tempura.

But not all of the dishes pack so much heat. A refreshing apricot kale salad is exactly what's needed to cool things down. And if onions or garlic aren't your thing, you're in luck; many menu items are marked onion- and/or garlic-free.

CLEAN BITES

- All sushi is made with brown rice and without sugar.
- No refined sugar is used in the kitchen.
- Menus vary slightly at each location.

SOTTO

9575 W. Pico Blvd.
310-277-0210

sottorestaurant.com
@sottoLA

As you descend the steps to this subterranean Italian eatery, you might feel like you're headed into a speakeasy. The lights are low, and the central wine vault is a reminder that the Italian good life often comes courtesy of what's in your glass. But "the goods" we care about in this case are the carefully crafted dishes bursting with fresh, seasonal ingredients.

To start, we're partial to the subtly smoky sautéed friarielli peppers, the succulent grilled pork meatballs paired with bitter greens and the blistered little gem lettuce salad. But don't fill up too much on small and medium plates—the main attractions are housemade pastas and authentic Neapolitan pizzas cooked in a hot-burning (over 900 degrees!), oak-fired oven. We especially love the sweet sausage and rapini pie with mild chilies.

For a lighter yet equally satisfying main dish, try the delightfully flaky whole grilled orata (sea bream). Molto bene!

CLEAN BITES

- Check Sotto's website to learn more about its purveyors.
- The pizza dough is composed of just four ingredients: water, flour, salt and yeast—but not of the commercial variety. Sotto exclusively uses biga, a natural starter, for a slow fermentation process.

Cuisine:
American
(Contemporary)

Neighborhood:
East Hollywood

Meals Served:
Breakfast, Brunch,
Lunch

SQIRL

720 N. Virgil Ave.　　　sqirlla.com
213-284-8147　　　　　@SQIRLLA

It may seem mind-boggling that people would stand in line for a half-hour for toast and jam, but if you've tasted owner Jessica Koslow's artisan preserves, you understand why. This is not mere bread topped with Smucker's, it's impossibly thick brioche slathered almost indecently with house-made, seasonal fruit conserves. (Santa Rosa plum chutney, anyone?)

Although jam put the tiny cafe on the map, there's much more on offer. Peruse the chalkboard menu as you queue alongside the open kitchen for the day's selections. High-quality ingredients elevate simple sandwiches like the pressed Beecher's cheddar with savory tomato jam and arugula on baguette.

More innovative dishes are truly masterful. The divine breakfast brown rice bowl pairs the grain with preserved Meyer lemon, lacto-fermented hot sauce, sorrel pesto, sheep feta and a poached egg. Addictive "kabbouleh" salad swaps crispy rice for traditional bulgur and shredded kale for parsley. Take a jar of jam to-go.

CLEAN BITES

- Ample vegetarian, vegan and gluten-free choices are clearly marked on the menu.
- The restaurant seeks out heirloom varieties of produce in the U.S. Ark of Taste that lists foods in danger of extinction.

SQUARE ONE DINING

4854 Fountain Ave.   squareonedining.com
323-661-1109

Cuisine:
American (Casual)

Neighborhood:
East Hollywood

Meals Served:
Breakfast, Brunch,
Lunch

If medals were given out for transparent sourcing, this cheery neighborhood cafe would win the gold. Just check under the "We Proudly Serve" section of its chalkboard menu and you're likely to find Chino Valley farm fresh eggs, Nueske smoked meats and Anson Mills grits, among other quality ingredients.

The kitchen takes equal care in preparing as in procuring them, and the result is fare that's rustic and gourmet at the same time. For breakfast (served all day!), the well-crafted omelets would get Julia Child's stamp of approval, while the fresh fruit bowl is a vibrant array of seasonal berries or stone fruit.

At lunch, salads are balanced and satisfying; each ingredient in the niçoise, from haricot vert to dijon-tarragon potatoes and house-cured tuna, is perfectly cooked. Sandwiches are also well-executed, especially the veggie club.

Waits can be lengthy, but scoring a seat on the breezy patio is divine.

CLEAN BITES

- Must try: For a carnivorous treat, get the hot, open-faced skirt steak sandwich with caramelized shallots.
- Check out Square One at the Boathouse in Echo Park, which offers a limited menu.

Cuisine:
Raw, Vegetarian/Vegan

Neighborhood:
Studio City

Meals Served:
Brunch, Lunch, Dinner

SUNCAFE

10820 Ventura Blvd.   suncafe.com
818-927-4100   @SunCafeOrganic

SunCafe is aptly named. The sharp, casual eatery recently moved into a bright new space on Ventura Boulevard, and the vibrant all-vegan fare exudes a sun-filled energy.

Although the food isn't groundbreaking, and you'll want to choose dishes with variety to avoid duplicated flavors, overall the meals are solid. We definitely appreciate the high-quality ingredients and colorful presentations.

Salads are gargantuan, like the appropriately named Kale Colossus. Pizzas come on granola-like raw crust that's crunchy yet chewy and surprisingly hefty. We were intrigued by the house-made "SunChorizo," a smoky, salty blend of sun-dried tomatoes and nuts. It proved delicious cradled in lettuce leaf tacos and crumbled over our Mexican pizza. The tempeh "bacon" BLT is also a safe, satisfying bet.

But we won't lie: The impressively thick and creamy kale shake—sweetened by cashews, bananas and agave—is SunCafe's No. 1 attraction.

CLEAN BITES

- Must try: kale shake.
- Almost everything is made from scratch, including burgers, chorizo, sauces, mayo and five kinds of seed/nut cheeses.
- SunCafe offers raw-food cooking classes every Saturday morning.

SUPERFOOD CAFE

530 Wilshire Blvd.   superfoodexpress.net
310-319-9100

Cuisine:
Californian

Neighborhood:
Santa Monica

Meals Served:
Breakfast, Lunch,
Dinner

Formerly known as Interim Cafe, this bright, order-at-the-counter venue split from its parent restaurant, Newsroom Cafe, in 2013 when it became Superfood Cafe. But the owner has preserved the same high-quality organic fare, with few changes to the wide menu, which features smoothies, organic egg dishes, sandwiches, salads and rice bowls.

The layered garden salads are an ideal way to get your daily dose of veggies. Our favorite is the Gado Gado—hemp tofu, snap peas, cucumber and sprouts mixed with tasty cashew dressing and a quinoa-brown rice medley. The zippy chicken masala salad, with Indian-spiced chicken and mango chutney vinaigrette, also won us over.

On the richer side, the fresh crab quesadilla is a worthy indulgence. Low-fat cheese and whole wheat tortillas make it slightly less guilt-inducing. Balance it with a light, fresh smoothie. We're partial to the Purple Erkle, featuring antioxidant-packed acai, blueberries and bananas with apple-pomegranate juice.

CLEAN BITES

- Must try: the organic, vegan soft serve ice cream.
- There's certainly something for everyone here. The menu is expansive!
- Gluten-free dishes are marked on the menu.

Cuisine:
American
(Contemporary)

Neighborhood:
Santa Monica

Meals Served:
Dinner

TAR & ROSES

602 Santa Monica Blvd.
310-587-0700

tarandroses.com
@TarAndRosesLA

This rustic-meets-urban hotspot is a love song to all things wood-fired. The smoky scent of smoldering wood wafts through the warmly lit room, an earthy juxtaposition to the after-work suit-and-cocktail-dress crowd that vies for one of the in-demand tables.

The contemporary small plates menu is heavy on high-quality meats like drool-worthy steaks and poultry, plus nose-to-tail offerings like braised lamb belly and bone marrow. (Wood roasting helps seal in the juices.) On the other hand, we happily found appetizers to be focused on Santa Monica Farmers Market-sourced vegetables, shifting with the seasons.

Also on the meatless tip, a luscious plate of lemony ricotta gnocchi with tender fava beans, spinach and asparagus left us scraping the bowl clean. And for pescetarians? Being close to the Pacific, it's hard to resist sampling the seafood. Forgo the shellfish pot and opt for the day's whole fish; our branzino was nothing short of spectacular.

CLEAN BITES

- Party of four or more? Order a week in advance for a T&R supper featuring a family-style three course meal.
- The wood used changes daily, alternating between walnut, oak, almond, apple and almond.
- Chef Andrew Kirschner previously did stints at other Clean Plates-approved restaurants: Joe's (p. 117), Wilshire (p. 166) and Axe (p. 72).

TAVERN

11648 San Vicente Blvd.   tavernla.com

310-806-6464

THE LARDER

Multiple locations

Cuisine:
American
(Contemporary)

Neighborhood:
Brentwood, Multiple
locations

Meals Served:
Breakfast, Brunch,
Lunch, Dinner

With several LA mainstays to her name (Lucques [p. 125], A.O.C. [p. 70], the Hungry Cat [p. 114]), celebrated chef Suzanne Goin opened Tavern in 2009. Her genius for selecting simple, top-quality ingredients and then letting them shine is on full display with Tavern's California Mediterranean menu.

Signature sandwiches like the Pilgrim (turkey layered with stuffing and cranberry) and the Styne (house-cured pastrami and gruyere) are some of the best in town. Organic turkey burgers defy dryness (tomato confit is mixed in the patty) and sweet potato chips are crisped to perfection.

Even the humble french fry seems to taste better here—golden yet soft on the inside, they're made with rice bran oil and many arrive with the skins still on. Seasonal sides showcase organic vegetables, like curried cauliflower that gets a zingy lift from red wine vinegar.

For a more budget-friendly experience, stop into the adjoining cafe and marketplace, The Larder, which serves many of the same lunch dishes and also offers to-go items. A huge hit, The Larder has three additional storefronts across town—hopefully one near you.

CLEAN BITES

- The Larder marketplace at Tavern's location features biodynamic wines, organically sourced provisions and to-go foods.

TENDER GREENS

Multiple locations

tendergreens.com
@TenderGreens

There may be long peak-hour lines and trays for carting your meal to your table, but the offerings at this quick-service, California-fresh chain bear little resemblance to classic cafeteria fare.

Forget chicken nuggets and tater tots, we're talking robust salads with locally sourced greens and seasonal vegetables, along with grilled, hormone- and antibiotic-free proteins. The vibe is farm stand meets eco-urban casual. Ogle the pristine ingredients and glimpse the rapid-fire speed of the cooks as the line snakes past the open kitchen.

Standout salads include the tuna nicoise (seared ahi with capers, olives and quail egg) and the Happy Vegan (tabbouleh, hummus and cucumber-beet quinoa). For a heartier fix, hot carved meats like juicy salt-and-pepper chicken—either tucked into sandwiches or plated with mashed potatoes—are supremely satisfying.

Want a healthier hot plate? Ask to swap mashed potatoes for roasted vegetables or salad.

CLEAN BITES

- Reclaimed, recycled and environmentally friendly materials are used for the interiors, and the work of local artists adorn the walls.
- Tender Greens started the Sustainable Life Project, which provides a work and learning environment to emancipated foster youth to help them transition into self-sufficient adulthood.
- Each location stars its own masterful chef.

TRUE FOOD KITCHEN

395 Santa Monica Place,
Suite 172
310-593-8300

truefoodkitchen.com
@TrueFoodKitchen

Cuisine:
Californian

Neighborhood:
Santa Monica

Meals Served:
Brunch, Lunch, Dinner

Is it possible to nourish your body at the mall? At this industrial-chic eatery set in Santa Monica Place, the answer is yes. The globally inspired menu is informed by principles of the anti-inflammatory diet courtesy of Dr. Andrew Weil, a partner in the restaurant.

While you can get a more memorable pizza at an Italian bistro or a more complex curry at a Thai restaurant, there's comfort in having confidence that the kitchen is cooking up healthy fats and proteins, whole grains and abundant fruits and veggies.

That doesn't necessarily mean you're sacrificing taste. Mint and lemon enliven the seasonal market salad; the heirloom tomato and watermelon salad is delightfully refreshing. Panang curry and shiitake lettuce cups prove satisfying without being heavy. We're impressed with the crisp, delicate, gluten-free crust option for the pizzas.

Whether you opt for a bison burger, fish dish or rice bowl, it's just what the doctor ordered.

CLEAN BITES

- Special dieters, rejoice: Vegan, vegetarian and gluten-free selections are clearly marked on the menu.
- The restaurant's environmentally conscious practices include high-efficiency kitchen equipment, reclaimed wood floors and Natura-purified water.
- The menu was created around the principles of Dr. Andrew Weil's anti-inflammation diet.

TUNING FORK

12051 Ventura Place
818-623-0734

Tuningforkgastropub.com
@TuningForkLA

Like most neighborhood watering holes, this lively gastropub is an ideal spot to grab a beer and some nibbles after work. But the seasonal, organic, health-minded comfort food sets it apart from your average bar.

Sure, there are wings and fries, yet it's easy to sidestep the bar snacks when the robust salads are so tempting. The chopped salad of baby artichokes and thinly sliced cucumber dressed in basil vinaigrette transported us to the Mediterranean. Perhaps our favorite dish, the quinoa bowl, was a savory mélange of multicolored quinoa, black beans, blistered cherry tomatoes and diced carrots.

The variety of meats and veggie-driven accompaniments elevate the burgers. We thrilled to the Gobbler, a turkey burger with arugula, onion marmalade and house ale mustard on a multigrain bun. Served with French lentils, butternut squash and Brussels sprouts, our grilled New York strip steak almost seemed too elegant for a pub.

CLEAN BITES

- Hooray for transparent sourcing! The local, sustainable, organic farmers and ranchers that supply the restaurant are name-checked on the website.
- Grass-fed beef and bison are the only kinds of beef and bison you'll find here.
- There are abundant vegetarian choices on the menu and several vegan ones, too—a rarity for a gastropub.

VENICE ALE HOUSE

2 Rose Ave.
310-314-8253

venicealehouse.com
@VeniceAleHouse

Cuisine:
American (Casual),
Gastropub

Neighborhood:
Venice

Meals Served:
Brunch, Lunch, Dinner

Against a true Venice Beach backdrop of street artists and rollerblading renegades, this indoor/outdoor beer garden right on the famed boardwalk pairs its brews with clean eats.

Bye-bye greasy bar snacks: Instead of wings and mozzarella sticks, this joint has farmers market-fresh guacamole with organic corn tortilla chips and "un-fries"—red potato wedges or sweet potato rounds roasted in sea salt, olive oil and coconut oil. Snappy veggies sautéed with garlic and almond slivers, as well as tomato-basil soup, also rank among our favorite starters.

Move on to robust entrée salads, plates of grilled local fish and customizable burgers with a bevy of healthy toppings like beet medallions and roasted red peppers. But the real measure of a Venice eatery is its taco, and here the veggie version—with sautéed button mushrooms, eggplant and zucchini—is excellent.

CLEAN BITES

- The kitchen uses sea salt, olive and coconut oil exclusively.
- Check out Venice Ale House's sister restaurant, Bank of Venice Public House.

Cuisine:
Californian,
Small Plates

Neighborhood:
Culver City

Meals Served:
Brunch, Lunch, Dinner

THE WALLACE

3833 Main St.
310-202-6400

thewallacela.com
@TheWallaceLA

The Wallace is a quirky-cool gem of a restaurant: The logo is an upside-down chair, and funky, mismatched art graces the walls. The Culver City Farmers Market sets up on the sidewalk out front—which is a big clue to The Wallace's guiding principle: fresh, seasonal produce.

Chef and owner Michael Teich (formerly at Axe [p. 72]) has created an innovative small plates menu. A whole section is devoted to novel "jarred" creations, including a warm roasted artichoke and crab dip that we relished with house-made root veggie chips.

The vegetable section proved the most voluminous and memorable. Shaved squash added bright color and texture to a market greens salad; creamy parmesan enriched charred cauliflower; and quinoa bejeweled with pomegranate seeds dressed up petite, Indian-spiced eggplant.

Proteins were also drive-across-town delicious, including flawlessly grilled pork belly and meaty scallops adorned with leeks and corn puree. Small portions encourage sharing—and portion control.

CLEAN BITES

- The Culver City Farmers Market sets up shop on the sidewalk out front on Tuesdays.
- Teich sources seafood that is approved as "safe and sustainable" by the Monterey Bay Aquarium.

WATER GRILL

544 S. Grand Ave.
213-891-0900

watergrill.com
@WaterGrill

1401 Ocean Ave.
310-394-5669

Cuisine:
Seafood

Neighborhood:
Downtown, Santa
Monica

Meals Served:
Lunch, Dinner

After more than 20 years of impeccable seafood service, Water Grill got both a design facelift and a menu makeover in 2012 that injected a more casual, contemporary ethos into the food and the vibe. Then, in 2013, it added an oceanfront location in Santa Monica. Despite the changes and expansion, the same flawless quality reigns.

The raw bar is still a highlight. Slurp down a selection of fresh oysters (the sampler allows you to try multiple varieties) accompanied by a trio of sauces.

You could almost make a meal of appetizers like crab cakes, shrimp bahn mi and grilled octopus. But save room for the incredible seafood plates, Water Grill's signature. Our standouts included the swordfish and Marine Stewardship Council-certified sea bass. Flavorful preparations, from Mediterranean to Asian, incorporate abundant seasonal veggies.

And all you landlubbers: Not to fear. There are a few chicken and meat dishes just for you.

CLEAN BITES

- We're cheerleaders for the transparent sourcing of produce and seafood here. You'll know if what you're getting is wild or farm raised.
- Water Grill launched the career of chef David LeFevre of MB Post (p. 129).

Cuisine:
American
(Contemporary)

Neighborhood:
Santa Monica

Meals Served:
Lunch, Dinner

WILSHIRE

2454 Wilshire Blvd.
310-586-1707

wilshirerestaurant.com
@WilshireRest

$$$

Wilshire's enchanting patio is one of its biggest draws. At night, fairy lights, candles and a glowing fireplace illuminate the sprawling space (with heat lamps in winter). The indoor bar scene is pretty electric, too.

We'd like to say the kitchen is also "on fire," but the food can admittedly be inconsistent. Still, with an emphasis on local, organic, seasonal ingredients, its heart is in the right place, and successful dishes erase any blunders from memory.

The fusion-style dishes marry American comfort food classics with European and Asian influences. Skip the ceviche but try the velvety black cod, which might be miso-marinated and accompanied by baby carrots, bok choy and shiitake mushrooms.

Local farmers markets determine what goes in salads and veggie sides. Simple preparations let the true flavors of the vegetables shine, from broccolini with a touch of chili heat to curried cauliflower sweetened with raisins.

CLEAN BITES

- Most dishes can be made without dairy or gluten.
- Try chef Sal Garcia's creations for only $5 to $7 during happy hour, 5 to 7 p.m., Monday through Saturday.

BEYOND RESTAURANTS

BAKERIES

BABYCAKES
Gluten-free, soy-free and and vegan cupcakes. All veggie-based food dyes for frosting.
236 N. Larchmont Blvd. | Larchmont | babycakesnyc.com

BREAKAWAY BAKERY
Gluten-free, kosher, whole-grain, dairy-free, soy-free, gum-free, nut-free pastries baked with coconut oil.
5264 W. Pico Blvd. | Mid-City | breakawaybakery.com

BUTTERCELLI BAKESHOP
Gluten-free, vegan, Paleo and whole-wheat options.
13722 Ventura Blvd. | Sherman Oaks | buttercelli.com

SWEETS FOR THE SOUL
Bakes with organic eggs, flour and spices.
3169 Glendale Blvd. | Atwater Village | sweetsforthesoul.com

ZEN BAKERY
Fiber rich, whole-grain cakes and muffins.
10988 W. Pico Blvd. | West LA | zenbakery.com

COFFEE SHOPS

ALFRED COFFEE & KITCHEN
Stumptown coffee and Farmshop sandwiches (see p. 100).
8428 Melrose Pl. A | Beverly Grove | alfredcoffee.com

BLACKTOP COFFEE

Serving Sight Glass beans, pressed juices and Guerilla tacos (see p. 170).

826 3rd St. | Downtown | blacktop.la

BRU COFFEEBAR

Single-origin and green beans from Ritual Coffee Roasters with outdoor seating and free internet.

1866 N Vermont Ave | Los Feliz | brucoffeebar.com

CAFECITO ORGANICO

Committed to developing relationships with its producers to ensure fair and sustainable practices.

Multiple locations | cafecitoorganico.com

CAFE DEMITASSE

Self-roasted beans from small producers that use organic fertilizers.

Multiple locations | cafedemitasse.com

CAFE DULCE

Organic and green beans from Lamill Coffee and unique pastries like the spirulina churro.

134 Japanese Village Plz Bldg E. | Downtown | cafedulce.co

CAFFE LUXXE

Single-origin coffee from small, independent farms and organic, biodynamic teas.

Multiple locations | caffeluxxe.com

COGNOSCENTI COFFEE

Offers beans from a few different roasters, all with a focus on eco-friendly, fair-trade farming practices. Guerilla tacos served (see p. 170).

6114 Washington Blvd. | Culver City | popupcoffee.com

GO GET EM TIGER

Forty Ninth Parallel coffee served with organic milk and house-made simple syrups.

230 N. Larchmont Blvd. | Larchmont Village | ggetla.com

GROUNDWORK

One of the first certified-organic tea and coffee roasters in Southern California.

Multiple locations | groundworkcoffee.com

INTELLIGENTSIA COFFEE

Direct-trade beans with a large wholesale program. Outdoor seating at some locations.

Multiple locations | intelligentsiacoffee.com

MENOTTI'S COFFEE SHOP

Four Barrel coffee and vegan treats.

56 Windward Ave. | Venice | menottis.com

PAPER OR PLASTIK CAFE

Single-origin, eco-friendly beans with a food menu featuring local and sustainable ingredients.

5772 W. Pico Blvd. | Mid-City | paperorplastikcafe.com

TOMS COFFEE BAR

Housed in the shoe company's Venice flagship shop, for every bag of direct-trade beans sold, it provides a week of clean water to a person in need.

1344 Abbot Kinney Blvd. | Venice | toms.com/coffee

TWO GUNS ESPRESSO

Caffe Vita coffee with organic milk options as well as organic teas.

350 N Sepulveda Blvd. | Manhattan Beach | twogunsespresso.com

FOOD TRUCKS

AMAZE BOWLS
Gluten-free and dairy-free acai bowls.
@amazebowls | amazebowls.com

GREEN TRUCK
Healthy meals on-the-go made with sustainably raised proteins, and local and organic produce. Vegan options.
@GreenTruck_LA | greentruckonthego.com

GUERILLA TACOS
Housed in Blacktop and Cognoscenti Coffee shops, tacos are made with thoughtfully procured proteins and farm-fresh produce.
@guerrillatacos | guerrillatacos.com

HEIRLOOM LA
Oft-changing menu always committed to supporting small, local, organic farms.
@heirloomla | heirloomla.com

JUICEBOX
Juicing local, organic produce to-go in a bio-diesel truck.
@juicebox | juiceboxlosangeles.com

LET'S BE FRANK
Grass-fed beef hotdogs with organic condiments.
@letsbefrank | letsbefrankdogs.com

ORGANIC OASIS
Raw, vegan ice cream.
@OrganicOasis | myorganicoasis.com

PLANT FOOD FOR PEOPLE

Local, organic, vegan fare.

@plantfoodforppl | plantfoodforpeople.moonfruit.com

VAN LEEUWEN

All ice cream is made with antibiotic- and hormone-free dairy. The vegan ice cream is soy-free and Toby's Estate coffee is on offer.

@VLAIC | vanleeuwenicecream.com

ICE CREAMERIES

BEACHY CREAM

Locally sourced, 100% organic ingredients. Large ice cream sandwich selection.

1209 Wilshire Blvd. | Santa Monica | beachycream.com

CARMELA ICE CREAM

Unique flavors of organic ice cream and sorbet made with farmers market produce.

Multiple locations | carmelaicecream.com

KINDKREME

Raw, vegan and organic frozen desserts.

Multiple locations | kindkreme.com

KIPPY'S!

Organic, coconut-based frozen desserts sweetened with raw honey.

326 Lincoln Blvd. | Venice | kippysicecream.com

MCCONNELL'S FINE ICE CREAMS

Small-batch ice cream made from grass-grazed milk and cream pasteurized at its own creamery. Ingredients are all local, sustainable and organic.

Multiple locations | mcconnells.com

PEDDLER'S CREAMERY

Organic ice cream churned by bicycle. Dairy-free options available.

458 S. Main St. | Downtown | peddlerscreamery.com

SWEET ROSE CREAMERY

Made with organic milk and eggs. Also offers dairy-free options.

Multiple locations | sweetrosecreamery.com

JUICE BARS

CLOVER JUICE BAR

Cold-pressed juices from sustainable, organic farmers along with some sandwich, salad and baked-good offerings.

Multiple locations | cloverjuice.com

EARTHBAR

Cold-pressed, 100% organic juices along with super-nutrient-concentrated Earthbar "shots."

Multiple locations | earthbar.com

EAGLE ROCK JUICE CO.

Freshly pressed, 100% organic juice to-go.

1565B Colorado Blvd. | Eagle Rock | eaglerockjuice.com

GLOW BIO

Probiotic-enhanced cold-pressed juices with 100% organic ingredients.

7473 Melrose Ave. | Fairfax | myglowbio.com

JUICE FARM

Smoothie and cold-pressed, organic juice bar with a solid selection of "boost" options.

36 W. Colorado Blvd., Suite 7 | Pasadena | juicefarmcoldpressed.com

JUICE SERVED HERE

100% organic, cold-pressed juices and raw, vegan and gluten-free desserts in eco-friendly packaging.

Multiple locations | juiceservedhere.com

KREATION JUICERY

Nutrient-dense snacks and 100% organic, cold-pressed juice sourced from local farmers markets.

Multiple locations | kreationjuice.com

LIQUID JUICE BAR

Family-owned organic juice bar with acai bowls.

8180 Melrose Ave. | Beverly Grove | liquidjuicebar.com

MOON JUICE

100% organic and cold-pressed juice shop and nut-milk bar with unique produce options.

Multiple locations | moonjuiceshop.com

ORCHARD FLATS

Multiple cold-pressed juice lines featuring root veggies and leafy greens as well as a line that supports honeybee health.

Multiple locations | orchardflats.com

THE PUNCHBOWL

Beautifully packaged cold-pressed juices, nut/seed milks and tonics.

4645 Melbourne Ave. | Los Feliz | lapunchbowl.com

SUSTAIN JUICERY

Cold-pressed, farm-fresh juices with some exotic produce options.

548 S. Spring St. #114 | Downtown | sustainjuicery.com

PROVISIONS

A CUT ABOVE
Butcher shop with grass-fed meats.
2453 Santa Monica Blvd. | Santa Monica | acabutchershop.com

ATWATER VILLAGE FARM
Organic, local produce at affordable prices.
3224 Glendale Blvd. | Atwater Village | atwatervillagefarm.com

BELCAMPO MEAT CO.
Full butcher shop along with counter-service meals. Specializes in grass-fed meats. Many grab-and-go items.
317 S. Broadway | Downtown | belcampomeatco.com

EREWHON MARKET
Cafe, grocery and juice bar.
7660 Beverly Blvd. | Fairfax | erewhonmarket.com

LINDY AND GRUNDY
Local, pastured and organic meats and butchery classes on-site.
801 North Fairfax Ave. | Fairfax | lindyandgrundy.com

MCCALL'S MEAT AND FISH CO.
Responsibly farmed and wild fish along with antibiotic- and hormone-free meats.
2117 Hillhurst Ave. | Los Feliz | mccallsmeatandfish.com

ORGANIX
Health food store with a juice bar, vegan deli and organic raw dairy for sale.
1731 Colorado Blvd. | Eagle Rock | organix-la.com

URBAN RADISH

Market featuring locally grown and organic produce, meats, poultry and seafood from ranchers who subscribe to ethical animal welfare standards, and dairy from small-batch producers.

661 Imperial St. | Downtown | urban-radish.com

WHOLE FOODS

There is plenty to choose from at this large supermarket chain that's committed to providing customers more natural and organic options as well as access to local products. Extensive produce section that demarcates local goods and a sizable bulk section. Serves as an incubator of sorts for local food start-ups.

Multiple locations | wholefoodsmarket.com

INDEX

NOTES

NOTES